Trial and Triumph
The Journey of a Military Brat

Ketia Swanier

By
Mary Cunningham

Copyright 2022 Ketia4Kids Foundation

ISBN 978-1-951543-16-7

All rights reserved. No part of this book may be reproduced or utilized in any form or by any means without permission in writing from the author. All requests should be addressed to the publisher.

Cover design by Colin Wheeler, MFA.
Wheelermotion.com

DANCING CROWS
PRESS

Dancing Crows Press
306 Huntington Drive
Temple, GA 30179

Dedicated to:

Military Brats,
my parents, Cornell & Rosie,
and my son, Jasper.

Ketia Swanier

Acknowledgements

First and foremost, to Ketia Swanier, for being the beautiful soul who inspired me with the hours and hours of interviews and personal stories that made this book possible. Your dedication, to improving the lives of Military Brats, is inspiring.

Heartfelt thanks to Rosie and Smokey Swanier for allowing me to extract your memories, precious photos, and deepest emotions for Ketia's biography. Time spent with you is a cherished gift.

To AAU coach, Mike Green, for talking with me for hours—inside—on a beautiful sunny day at Mirror Lake Country Club. Memories of Ketia, both on and off the basketball court, were invaluable to the completion of this biography.

Much appreciation to Jim "Mr. Jim" Nichols, founder of The Georgia Magic, AAU, for sharing priceless insights from the first time you saw Ketia dribble a basketball, through the present. And, for being willing to share the results (and picture) of a couple of questionable, but rewarding bets you made with the team.

To Tonya Cardoza, Temple Head Women's Basketball Coach, for writing the warm and genuine foreword for the book. Respect for, and involvement in, Ketia's career and well-being, came through loud and clear.

Much gratitude goes to Dancing Crows Press and Editor, Elyse Wheeler, for making this book a reality. Your time, dedication, and generosity to the Ketia4Kidz Foundation are immeasurable in sharing Ketia's story with the world.

To all the fabulous writers in the Carrollton Writers Guild for your critiques, encouragement, and laughs along the way. (Remember when you all dozed off as I read a particularly boring chapter draft?)

Last, but not least, to my patient husband, Ken, whose technical and creative advice is always there when I need it, most.

Foreword

I was pleasantly surprised, but delighted, when I received a request from Ketia Swanier to write a brief foreword for her book, ***Trial and Triumph: The Journey of a Military Brat.***

While still an assistant at UConn, I had the pleasure of getting to know Ketia in the recruiting process, not only as a player but a person. It goes without saying, her parents, Rosie and Smokey Swanier did a tremendous job! Ketia made my job easy because she wanted to get better every year. She was a joy to be around, and was always respectful. As a student athlete, it is not easy with all the demands placed upon you, but because of her upbringing, Ketia was quickly able to adjust/adapt with whatever situation she faced.

So, it doesn't surprise me that she has now taken the time out to give back and impart some insight on how being a child of military parents and an elite athlete, at the highest level, has helped shaped her life.

The story of Ketia Swanier, her drive and determination, her career-military parents, and loyal support system, will not disappoint! I could think of no one better, to share their story of a positive outcome in the face of many challenges. She conveys hope to those in similar circumstances. During times of trial and sorrow, you may rise. And if you truly believe in yourself, and have the right people in your corner, anything is possible!

Now, as the Head Coach for Temple University, I look back on my days at UConn and can only hope I was someone Ketia could come to for anything, and that I played a positive part in the woman she is today.

Tonya Cardoza

UConn assistant coach from 1994-2008.
Temple head coach from 2008 to present.
2011 Atlantic Coast Conference Coach of the Year.

Prologue

She pulled the hood over her head and shoved nearly-frozen hands into the pouch of her sweatshirt. *The States never felt like this.* The temperature hadn't been above -10 for over a week, and the lack of adequate insulation in the gymnasium did little to moderate the bone-chilling temperature.

Her mind drifted to the past summer; drinking a cold glass of sweet tea on her mom and dad's West Georgia deck, taking in the warmth of the sun, until a shiver, running the full length of her spine, interrupted the warm memory. She took her hands from their cozy nest, cupped them together and blew hot air into her palms. "On second thought," she grumbled, "replace that iced tea with a steaming cup of hot cocoa."

She was the first one to arrive for morning practice, so the gym was even colder than usual without the dozen, or so, warm bodies running wind sprints across the hardwood floor. She grabbed her gloves, shoved a knit cap over her short-cropped hair, replaced the hood, and did a couple of easy stretches. The chilled air was unfavorable for much of a warmup. Ever since she reached the ripe old age of thirty, she'd become more cautious about overextending her muscles and joints. Ankles, once considered strong and capable of handling leaps, split-second changes of direction, and dogged defense, were now carefully wrapped to prevent injury. One ankle sprain last year gave her such a scare, taping had become a necessary precaution. She sighed, longing for her early twenties when she'd first entered the pros. Strength and stamina was taken for granted.

Any minute now, some of her younger teammates would bounce inside, put on their sneakers, and start warmups; even in a gym that could've easily doubled as her mom's freezer. Resentment, about her age or theirs, however, was not an option. Not in the mind of Naketia Marie Swanier, known as Ketia or "Keesh" to her family, friends, and the basketball world.

She glanced at her watch and wondered how soon the other American players would arrive with the trainer. None had learned to drive typical Eastern European stick shift cars, so catching a ride was imperative. At least she had arrived before Amanda, one of her American teammates, who had the uncanny ability to anticipate Ketia's arrival before she even entered the gym.

"Hey Keesh," she often heard her teammate call from inside the closed door.

"How'd you know it was me?" Ketia would ask, even though she'd get the same answer, every time.

"I know your footsteps," Amanda laughed. The answer puzzled Ketia because she'd always considered herself light on her feet; practically walking on her toes.

Ori was Ketia's first coach when she arrived in Rybnik Poland. They'd been separated for eight years while she played for other teams, so when he moved to the head coaching position in Sosnowiec, (Sos-no´-vich) Ketia was the first player he called. "Ketia, you come play for me." There was never a doubt in her mind that she would honor his *request*.

It was anyone's guess when he'd get to practice that day. He was always late. It could be a few minutes or a half hour. Hard to tell. Ketia's habit for punctuality was one of the most difficult routines to overlook in others, especially after spending college years under a coach and system that thrived on discipline and reliability. Not to mention the early years spent watching her mom and dad adhere to strict military discipline while integrating their daughter into the same system.

No sense getting impatient. She'd learned, years ago, Ori operated on his own time schedule. Wishing he'd be on time was an exercise in futility. Instead, she would often make a game of trying to guess how he'd run practice, once he got there. She dared not hope it would be anything but incredibly boring; stressing quantity over quality. After her intense learning process over four years at The University of Connecticut under Geno Auriemma, she'd come to the conclusion there wasn't too much more to learn from overseas coaches. After all, how do you improve on one of the most respected names in college basketball?

She did some easy hamstring stretches and reflected how group energy had picked up the past couple of weeks with the addition of three-on-three drills. While she'd been less than eager to get started that chilly morning, at least that type of practice had a purpose and helped shape teamwork. It also created far more competition than her coach's favorite drill, wind sprints. Ketia had always thrived on competition, from T-Ball to AAU to college and now the pros.

Although most of her teammates spoke good English, the coach's grasp on the language was questionable, at best. Whenever he wanted them to move faster, he'd yell, "Gas! Gas! Gas!" During practice or a game, he could be heard ordering, "Pass to the Ketia! Pass to the Ketia!" No matter how many times she'd heard that, it always brought a chuckle.

Ori had his light-hearted side, too. After practice, they could count on him to entertain with his latest dance moves. Oh, how he loved to dance. The joy on his face, during spirited twists and spins, was easily transferred to all his players; whether native-born or international.

Ketia moved to the bleachers and reflected on the huge banner hanging on the opposite side of the gym. There she was, larger than life, wearing *Number 11*; the number she'd worn through college, and most of her pro career. The guard from America had become one of the most recognizable faces of Polish basketball. A tribute to her popularity among the small, but loyal group of fans who cheered for her week after week, the banner showed her with basketball in hand; arm draped across the shoulder of her teammate, Ola. Far different from when she first moved to Poland and residents would stare at her brown skin making her feel like an oddity or an alien. She'd wondered at the time, if moving, alone, to a foreign country was a smart idea. With each passing year, however, she had made her mark on the basketball court and even learned to take in stride, and embrace, her *celebrity* status, along with the country's culture. Soon, she found herself staring at other persons of color because there were, still, so few in the country.

Getting to the stage of comfort for things she could control, and acceptance for things she couldn't, had been a long, sometimes arduous path. She'd been forced, over the years, to summon her inner strength in order to battle loneliness and fear.

"Ketia!" So deep in thought, she hadn't noticed the team and coaches arriving. In Polish-accented English, one asked, "Are you going to stare at your giant portrait all morning, or join us for practice?"

Everyone laughed, including Ketia. "I've been waiting on you. Let's get this party started!"

Being a military brat means being unique, strong, independent, and adaptable

—Military Brat

Chapter One: The Early Years

Playtime in the backyard was fun and, typically, uneventful. That particular morning, however, would be remembered, decades later, for a frightening event that almost turned deadly.

A colony of ants, marching up and down a nearby tree, captivated the two young cousins. They watched, with glee, while hundreds of the tiny red creatures marched up and down the trunk on a mesmerizing quest. The intrigue ended when it became frighteningly apparent the insects had changed direction and were continuing their mission up the legs of the small girls!

"Hundreds of Mississippi fire ants swarmed over us," Ketia recalled. She wasn't quite sure why the memory was still vivid, but traumas are not easily forgotten, even at such a young age. When her older cousin, Dana, pulled her up from the ground, it was obvious the three-year-old had been "ground zero" in the ant parade. "I had dozens of tiny red bites all over me. Thinking about it still freaks me out to this day."

The moment Rosie comprehended the scene unfolding, her screams echoed through the neighborhood as she sprinted across the yard toward the red swarm marching, resolutely, over her daughter's small body. Military training, blending with *mother's instinct,* kicked into high gear. Although it only took seconds for her to reach the screaming child, she remembered mentally mapping out the best route to the hospital as she ran.

It was evident Ketia took the worst of the bites. Dana, a little older and with much less discomfort, helped wipe the swarming insects from the toddler's legs and rush inside with her aunt to get Ketia in the tub. Fire ant bites are extremely painful to adults, but they can be deadly to children. Dana sat, wide-eyed on the bathroom floor; frightened for her little cousin.

Rosie held her breath as she washed the deadly creatures off her daughter's skin and down the drain. Ketia calmed down as the cool water soothed her skin. After a careful examination, miraculously, she was left with only minor bites. In fact, the child couldn't quite figure out the frightened looks on the faces of her mother and cousin.

Rosie scooped her daughter from the tub, dried her with a towel, and held on tight. A little *too* tight. "I can't breathe Ketia insisted. "I'm okay, mommy. You can let go."

At a young age, Ketia instinctively took over the role as comforter. Her transformation, that day, from sheer panic to composure, became a trait she would rely on from that time forward; an inner strength to be okay, no matter how dire the circumstances. There was also no doubt about the youngster's resolve to provide reassurance to those around her.

Strength and resolve would be a cornerstone throughout Ketia Swanier's life for one main reason. "Good luck asking me where I'm from," she'd comment to friends, peers, and the media. "I moved six times before college; Louisiana, Germany, Louisiana again, Texas, back to Germany and then to Georgia. In other words, everywhere." The ability to adapt, no matter how sudden or difficult the next move proved to be, would serve her well. She learned from the best after witnessing that quality, throughout the years, in her parents.

Cornell (Smokey) and Rosie Swanier were both dedicated to a career in the military. They met in Korea in the same unit in Dongducheon, Camp Casey, Korea, where

First Sergeants, Rosie and Cornell (Smokey)

a persistent young soldier found every excuse imaginable to drop by the armament room. He couldn't help but notice the tall, striking young woman working there assigning weapons to the troops.

After several vague conversations initiated by Smokey, Rosie had to find out from her roommate that the young, handsome private liked her and wanted to pursue a relationship. "Now, why didn't he just come out and ask me?" Rosie, outgoing and direct, had no way of knowing how shy and painfully homesick her admirer was at the time.

Both in their early 20's, it didn't take long for their mutual love of sports to inspire an instant connection, even though his interests were softball and football and hers was basketball. Friendship soon turned to love and they were married, in Monterey, California, in November, 1983.

After a thirteen-month tour in Fort Ord, California, they returned to Korea. In addition to training duties, Smokey was recruited into a fast-pitch softball league that took him all over the country. Rosie traveled with him as the team's one and only fan. Since he was stationed at the Demilitarized Zone and she was headquartered in Seoul, an hour-and a half bus ride away, her ability to accompany the team gave them precious time together, along with the opportunity to visit some of the nicer bases and picturesque areas of South Korea.

Neither had ever questioned their career choices, even after Ketia was born two years into their marriage. Although they had since moved back to the States, life, admittedly, got more complicated with the addition to their family. No matter what the military threw at them, they had no choice but to adapt and take it in stride, as did their child.

Weeks after Ketia's birth in Fort Polk, Louisiana, August 10, 1986, she flew, with her mother, from Louisiana to Georgia to visit her maternal grandmother, Ann, in Sandersville; the first of many plane trips for the youngster.

A trip several years later produced one of her best memories of those Georgia visits. During frequent errand runs, her Uncle Sam would put Ketia in his lap and let her pretend she was driving. "How many kids can say they started driving at age four," she laughed. A later trip to Walmart, with her uncle, also produced her first bike. "Purple, I think. That was my first taste of independence." That independence came with a price, though. Her mother insisted she wear a helmet to which Ketia complained, bitterly. "No helmet, no bike," Rosie commanded. End of discussion.

When she was two, the family moved to Wiesbaden, Germany where she was enrolled in daycare at Lindsey Air Station while both parents worked. "They'd set their alarm for 03:30. Mine was set for the same time." As most military brats learned, life was as regimented for them as their parents'. No fuss. No complaining.

While Ketia slipped into the role with apparent ease, Smokey and Rosie had the burden of their individual careers, along with the added responsibility of raising a child. Their goal was to give their daughter the best of both worlds. While they'd signed up for the military, Ketia was pulled along through necessity. They were determined to make her childhood years as normal as possible.

Normalcy, however, didn't come easy, nor did teaching Ketia the fine line between self-sufficiency and safety.

Although her parents wanted her to be confident and self-assured, her independent streak nearly led to

Ready to take on the world.

disaster. Smokey planned a trip with Ketia to a neighborhood video store, in Wiesbaden, Germany, to choose a movie for the evening's entertainment. While her dad wandered around the main store, Ketia, on a mission, ducked into the children's section to search. She found her favorite *Care Bears* tape, tucked it under her arm, crawled under the security door, and walked straight out of the store. Crossing several busy streets on the way home, she bounced in the front door of her home, eager to get movie night started.

"Where's your dad," Rosie asked the moment Ketia popped the video in the player. "I guess he's still at the video store," the four-year-old answered, unconcerned. A few minutes later, Smokey burst breathlessly through the front door, his face ashen with fear; tears streaming down his face. "I lost Ketia," he cried. Rosie's initial reaction was to keep him "on the hook" for taking his eyes off his daughter, but after seeing the anguish on his face she knew he'd suffered enough. "She's here. She walked home by herself."

Smokey slumped into the chair.

Decades later, he recalled the terror of that day. "I had everyone in the store looking for her. We started a search party. The fear in my heart was crushing."

After that, Ketia's parents determined the need to keep a more vigilant watch over their adventurous daughter without inhibiting her free spirit.

A year later, it was necessary to send Ketia back to the states for six months to live with her Mississippi grandparents. Tensions in the Middle East, and the launching of Desert Storm, created circumstances so unstable, it was determined she'd be safer back home in the States. While it was a tough decision, it would be the first and last time she had to live without at least one parent. From then on, for their daughter's sake, and their peace of mind, the Swaniers made sure one of them would be home at all times.

Ketia, age five, flew to Pass Christian, Mississippi to the home of paternal grandparents, Adrian and Corena Swanier. "To leave her was difficult," Rosie remembered, "but she was happy to be with her grandparents because she could finally get away with everything." Although that wasn't really the case, Ketia was a joy to her grandparents.

Army support requirements dictated children must have an optional place to live when there was the possibility both parents could be deployed at the same time. Rosie was on duty 24/7, so their choices were already limited. If Smokey was required to go to Kuwait, they wanted to know that their daughter was settled with the least amount of last-minute trauma. For most five-year-olds, leaving their parents and moving to another country would've been upsetting, but even at that tender age Ketia was used to relocating and changing schools. That didn't stop her from begging her mom to take her on the plane when Rosie flew back to Germany. Rosie was heartbroken to leave her daughter. Knowing it was for Ketia's own good didn't make the separation any easier.

On the bright side, Ketia was fortunate to be able to attend the same school in which her grandmother taught fourth grade. This made the transition easier for the kindergartener since it was the first time she'd had to adapt to life without either of her parents.

Ketia's time in Mississippi was made more enjoyable when her Uncle Virgil, or Uncle Red as he was known, was around to help take care of her. He always made it a special point to include his niece when he ran errands. Ketia loved having him around, but, once again, had to accept people coming in and out of her life when, after a few weeks visit, he went back to California. She cried "a rainstorm" after he left because she missed him so much.

Love and loss were two emotions she was forced to learn at an early age. Before one move back to America, she wasn't allowed to take her parakeet, Corky, with her, so finding a good home for him was a priority. Also, a priority was learning to accept loss, once again.

Along with her grandmother teaching at the elementary school, Ketia's grandfather was principal at the local high school. He was a quiet man, but as those who knew him said, "When Adrian Swanier spoke, people listened." In fact, almost two decades later, his words would practically lift him to prophet status in his Mississippi coast community.

**First Grade, Ketia, 2nd row
in front of her favorite teacher, Mrs. Davis.**

A move back to Fort Polk, Louisiana in 1992, where she'd been born six years earlier, meant adapting, once again, to a new school, friends, and schedule. She attended First Grade at Rosepine Elementary School where she met her "first ever favorite teacher, Mrs. Davis." Ketia still remembers receiving the "Math-a-thon" honor award. After school, she played with other kids at the Maw Maw and Paw Paw Daycare Center until her mother or dad picked her up.

Ketia was the only girl on the T-League team

This was also when she had her first experience with team sports; T-Ball. "My dad played underhand fast-pitch when we were in Germany, so my interest came naturally." The game didn't come easy for her, though. She played third base and struggled when it came to catching fly balls. Her team was on defense and up by one run in the last inning. There were two outs. "The batter hit a pop fly straight towards me. Before I could worry about not catching the ball, it plopped in my glove and the team celebrated like we'd won the World Series."

Her experiences off the field, however, would affect the six-year-old in a new and unexpected way. While Ketia loved every minute she was *on* the field, *off* the field activities and relationships would test her resolve.

She formed a friendship with a little girl who lived down the street. One day, the new friend asked Ketia to come to her house. They spent the afternoon, playing outside. Not long after it started to rain, Ketia walked back home, her clothes soaking wet. When questioned by Rosie about her playtime and why she was so wet, all she said was, "We had fun." Her mother suspected something was wrong, but let it drop.

The family of the little girl would often pass the Swanier house on their bikes. "They'd go on rides, together," Ketia observed. "I'd watch each one pass by, without speaking or acknowledging my existence."

It wasn't until much later that Ketia admitted to her mother, even during torrential rain, she hadn't been allowed to go inside her friend's house. "She said it's because I'm black." Young Ketia couldn't understand why her friend's mom would make that distinction when no one else in her life ever had. "Am I black? I didn't even know I was a color." Rosie was crushed by her words. Until that time, Ketia had never thought about being different from anyone else. Her parents taught her she was *no more or no less important than anyone on earth.*

When asked by her Rosie why she didn't talk about the incident when it happened, Ketia maintained, "Because I knew exactly what you'd do."

Years later, Rosie admitted that her daughter's discretion was probably the best course of action at the time. "She knows me all too well. At least she didn't allow an ugly and mean situation to make *her* react ugly and mean." Ketia also didn't allow the incident to test her mother's response.

SWANIER, Nakelia Marie, g.: 1. hobbies are stamps & baseball 2. favorite food is macaroni & cheese 3. is very good at playing baseball 4. likes to spend free time playing basketball 5. wants to be a basketball player when she grows up 6. was born in Louisiana

**Third Grade bio was spot on
(Note from teacher)**

Life is always changing, and if you don't learn to adjust, you will be left behind.

— Military Brat

Chapter Two: Love, Loss, and Friendship

Soon after a move to Fort Hood, Killeen, Texas in 1993, a friend of the family introduced the Swanier's to a German Shepherd/Chow mix in need of a good home. It was love at first sight for Ketia, although she didn't dare get too excited since pets had never been discussed in a positive way. She was surprised and thrilled, however, when her parents agreed to the new addition.

It wasn't known how long the dog had been wandering, alone, but the poor thing looked like she hadn't eaten a decent meal for months by the outline of her visible ribs.

The first order of business, for Ketia, was giving her new friend a proper name. A prominent, dark brown shape on the dog's back gave the imaginative child an idea. "I decided on 'Diamond'." As Ketia watched the dog eagerly devour two packs of hotdogs, she had visions of entering her new "friend" in a hotdog-eating competition and winning millions for herself and her family. *Diamond might even get his own diamond-encrusted collar! Hey, a girl and her dog can dream.*

Besides the excitement of a new family member, the result of the Texas move would produce a life changing event. It was there she met Khadija Talley. "We had so much in common, right from the beginning. Khadija was the sister I never had," Ketia recalled. "The first time we hung out there was an immediate connection. It felt like we met at birth and had known each other every day since then."

As it turned out, Ketia's instincts were spot on. The two six-year-old friends had more in common than they realized.

Through casual conversations among their parents, an amazing connection was discovered. Khadija and Ketia, both only children, were born just days apart in the same hospital. "Her birthday is eight days after mine, both in August, 1986. Her dad was military and my parents were military. It was one of those 'it's a small world' moments."

The two became fast friends. If both Ketia's parents were away, she'd stay at the Talley house. In turn, Khadija would stay with the Swaniers until her parents got home from work in the evening. They were inseparable the whole time their families lived at Fort Hood.

In addition to fulfilling her dream to have a dog, and meeting her life-long friend, that first year at Fort Hood brought a gift that would, forever, shape the direction of her life. Ketia had picked up her basketball one Saturday morning when she and her dad were in the garage. To his amazement, she started dribbling it between her legs. "Daddy, is this how you're supposed to do it?" The broad grin on Smokey's face said it all.

After that day, there was no doubt what her 7th birthday present would be; her first Playschool basketball goal. "It came so naturally," Ketia recalled. "My parents said I dribbled the ball so much, that's all they heard in their sleep."

An excellent basketball player in her own right, Ketia's mother, Rosie, had played college ball at Savannah State, in Georgia. After college, she enlisted in the Army and went on to play intramural basketball on various Army bases. She took seven-year-old Ketia with her to practice and expected her daughter to sit on the bleachers, watch the repetitive drills, and probably get bored. Bored? Not the enterprising youngster. The bleachers were empty. Ketia found a basketball and had staked her claim at the opposite end of the gym; making shot after shot. Rosie's teammates took notice, too. Like mother, like daughter. Basketball talent was definitely in the genes.

Rosie was also the one who taught Ketia the butterfly; a dribbling exercise designed to help with hand-eye coordination. To Rosie's delight, even after Ketia perfected the drill, she, again, wouldn't stop dribbling. That's when Rosie knew her young daughter had a special gift along with the drive to perfect it.

Basketball, however, wasn't the only sport that interested young Ketia. Rosie had no trouble spotting the days her daughter accompanied Smokey to softball or flag football practice. An incredibly muddy pair of shoes gave their father/daughter exploits away. Putting up with a little dirt, Rosie knew, was small price to pay. Ketia loved hanging out with the guys from her dad's company and they, in turn, loved and appreciated her athletic abilities. They never tired of watching her throw a football, play baseball, or display lightning-fast running skills. Anyone, the least bit sports-minded, knew they were witnessing the maturing of a first-class athlete.

Ketia followed her dad's love of baseball.

Ketia was fortunate to get her natural basketball ability and drive from her mom, and her athletic aptitude and speed from her dad. That, along with her love of the sport, emerging confidence, and work ethic, added up to a winning combination.

When Ketia and Khadija were nine, they played, together, on an intramural basketball team. "That was my first experience with team ball. I sucked because my love of baseball came from my dad. I just wanted to play my own game. On a team, I had to learn the rules and the concepts." Fortunately, both girls thrived during the experience.

As was always the case with the military, however, the inevitable move would send the best friends to different parts of the world. It would be six years before they reconnected. In 1999, while the Swanier's were assigned to Fort Benning, Georgia, Ketia flew to Fort Sill, Lawton, Oklahoma to stay with the Talley family. "Dad was deployed, at the time, and Mom had to spend three weeks training at the First Sergeant's Academy at Fort Bliss, Texas. No problem. I stayed with Khadija."

Neither girl had to wonder about the other's view of life. They were both military brats with the same anxieties and fears. Besides that, their relationship went beyond friendship, straight into a sisterhood of understanding.

"It was very cool of our parents to recognize the importance of visiting each other. When we hung out it was like we were never apart. We stayed up half the night eating Oreo Cookies and playing video games." Ketia called that one of her best childhood memories, especially since the pair didn't speak nearly as much after college. Still, both girls knew their friendship would continue no matter how long they were separated.

Today, Khadija helps a ton with the non-profit, Ketia4Kidz. She aides with choosing scholarship applications, along with organizing the recipient side of the non-profit foundation.

During their time at Fort Hood, Ketia's parents also enrolled her in Taekwondo to build her confidence and

Ketia and Khadija on the way to the prom

character. Years later, she lamented the fact that she never got her black belt. "Once I'd reached that level, it was time to pack up and move, again."

After three years in Texas, the next tour for the Swanier family required a move back to Germany. Again, the child had to face loss; this one, sudden and heartbreaking.

Her beloved dog, Diamond, had become her best friend; almost a sibling, since she was an only child. Ketia arrived home from school and, as usual, headed to the backyard calling, "Diamond! Diamond!" The cute doghouse, built especially for her pup, was empty, so she ran inside; again calling, "Diamond, Diamond!" The dog was nowhere in sight. She cried and cried until it occurred to her that moving a dog to Germany wasn't an option.

Although her parents were heartbroken for their daughter, they knew she'd have to accept the loss and move on. No questions were asked and no explanation was ever given. Just another lesson on how life had to be. "I didn't even get the opportunity to say goodbye. I tear up to this day, every time I tell the story."

Her mom never let her get another dog after Diamond even though she always begged for one. Deep down she knew the family didn't have the time to give a dog the attention it deserved. Besides, Ketia realized her mom would be the main person in the family taking care of a pet; an extra responsibility Rosie didn't need on her plate. "She did buy me a hamster when I was 14 years old, probably to get me off her back about a dog, but I never got over losing Diamond."

After the move back to Germany, the family would face another type of challenge.

Her parents were adamant that their daughter's physical and emotional needs always come first, even though it was incredibly hard on them to take turns running a single-parent household. While Rosie endured fewer deployments than Smokey, he had more challenges adapting to being the single parent; a challenge that would soon be tested. After their move in 1996, Rosie was ordered to deploy from Germany to Bosnia for eleven months.

"I'll never forget the day she left," Smokey recalled. "We were stationed in Wurzburg, lived in Giebilestadt, Germany and I worked just outside the gate about two miles from the small Kasern; German for military installation."

"Believe it or not, my biggest worry, at the time, was Ketia's hair!" Caring for a little girl's hair is challenging for the most experienced father. Having never been in the position of hair stylist, Smokey was lost. He finally enlisted the help of another military mom who agreed to wash and style Ketia's hair once every two weeks. Through perseverance and much trial and error, he finally mastered the art of braiding. Whew! *One problem off the list.*

For Smokey, single parenting was one of the most demanding aspects of his life. At the same time Rosie was in Bosnia, he was in charge of about 30 soldiers in a detachment away from the main company. For the most part, due to ultimate control, he had free rein when it came to his schedule. "It also helped to have well-trained and experienced non-commissioned officers on call," he conceded. Most of all, he was grateful to have the flexibility to be home when his daughter needed him.

With her mom deployed, Ketia had grown into a resilient ten-year-old. After school she'd get off the bus, go home and call her dad to let him know she was safely inside. Since the community was gated, with neighbors close by, he didn't have to worry about her security. If he couldn't leave work early to cook dinner, he made sure his daughter had leftovers.

Although hair issues were under control, and Ketia's routine had normalized, Smokey still worried. Would his daughter's school work and grades suffer? *Mom* had always been the stickler when it came to education. Now, *Dad* would have to take over that duty. To Smokey's great relief, it never became a concern because Ketia would fix a snack and then dive into her homework as soon as she got home from school. "What eleven-year-old does that without being told?" He shook his head in amazement recalling those months they were both without Rosie's steady influence.

It was clear then, Ketia was an eleven-year-old who learned, at an early age, to accept responsibility.

"She was the true meaning of what a military brat was made of, resilient, adaptive, and high character," he observed, proudly.

Ketia was, naturally, deep into sports during that time. On holidays or summer, when school was out, she'd go to work with her dad on activity days, and do physical training with the other soldiers. To her delight, many of those days included basketball games. Smokey could see how much she thrived while shooting hoops in the gym for hours at a time.

In fact, all who observed the young athlete appreciated her skills. "My soldiers were impressed with her dribbling and her ability to push the ball up and down the floor."

While basketball was her main focus, soccer came in a close second, and like a true athlete, she was very good. Smokey signed her up to play on a nearby team in order to keep her busy. During one phone call to her mother, she described the technique. "It's just like playing basketball, only with my feet."

Ketia loved soccer almost as much as basketball

Although her destiny was to excel at basketball, she regretted the decision not to pursue soccer because, to this day, she believes she would've had a good chance to make the United States Olympic team. She loved the sport so much, she never let Smokey live down the fact that he wouldn't buy her soccer cleats. "I ended up playing in the same high-top Nike's I used for softball!" Despite the lack of "proper footwear", she was exciting to watch; as swift with her feet as she was dribbling a basketball.

Playing sports wasn't her only passion, however. She played saxophone in the school band and became so good, that she vowed to continue playing when time allowed. Never could she have imagined that chance wouldn't come again until she was well into adulthood. Basketball, track, soccer, and school occupied her to the point she found few quiet moments to participate in her love of music. Describing Ketia Swanier as "well-rounded" was an understatement.

After Rosie completed her deployment to Bosnia, and returned to the base in Germany, the family had *two whole months* together until Smokey deployed to Saudi Arabia. All too soon, the Swanier family was, again, down to two; this time, mother and daughter.

Even with both parents present, adapting to life on a military base was difficult for a curious, active child. Smokey and Rosie discovered there were simply no programs, entertainment, or activities for kids. They fought to get their daughter into organized sports activities with kids her own age; however, girl's teams were few and far between. Ketia had also grown weary of being bullied by the girls because she played sports with the boys during recess.

Intramural Basketball in Germany

Observing her continuing love and aptitude for basketball, Smokey and Rosie had the foresight to sign her up for intramural ball in Germany, even though she had to play with boys since there weren't enough girls, her age, signed up to meet team requirements. That road block turned out to be a blessing in disguise. Her skills accelerated during that time, and soon, she was running circles around the boys.

It wasn't long before a joint decision was made by her parents and coaches that she was good enough to play with older girls (ages 13-15) on a junior league that traveled around Germany playing at other military installations. Despite her athletic ability, getting her on the team wasn't an easy task because of her young age. They encountered all kinds of road blocks until the base support commander saw her play. While talking to Smokey after one of Ketia's games, he found out the difficulty of their mission to get her on the older team. Fortunately, for the Swaniers, and the basketball world, it didn't take long for the commander to take notice of her talent and get her in the girl's league.

Age 11, Ketia held her own with older girls

Finally, Ketia would have the opportunity to be tested by players with equal skills. The older girls were excited to have her on the team and knew, by the reputation preceding her; the 11-year-old could hold her own. And, she did. At the end of the season, the team made it to the finals of the United States Army Europe Championships after which Ketia received the tournament sportsmanship award.

The Amateur Athletic Union's mission statement is: To offer amateur sports programs through a volunteer base for all people to have the physical, mental, and moral development of amateur athletes, and to promote good sportsmanship and good citizenship.

Chapter Three - AAU (Sports for all, forever)

In Germany, Ketia loved the challenge of playing on teams with boys, or teams consisting of older girls. Despite the gender and age difference, her natural ability out-paced the competition. After watching a few games on the base, a soldier in Rosie's unit, Master Sergeant Smith, known as "Smitty", suggested they check out AAU (Amateur Athletic Union) in the States.

After some serious sleuthing, Smokey discovered AAU's purpose was to create a venue in which kids from 9-18 can play competitive sports in their local communities, regionally, and nationally to strengthen their skill level. It sounded perfect! If they could get Ketia in the organization, she'd, for once, be able to play with peers of equal talent. She'd also have the fun of traveling to other parts of the United States for tournaments; a good preview of what she'd face in college—practice, tight schedules, and tons of basketball!

He was also pleased to learn that tournaments were typically a gathering place for college scouts. Getting Ketia into a national recruiting conversation, as soon as possible, would increase her chances of going to a highly ranked school.

As the Swaniers were about to find out, the cost and disruption could be a heavy burden to the family of any AAU, or extramural participant. They were no exceptions, especially with the logistical and financial addition of flying Ketia back and forth from Germany to the States.

After a family conference, Smokey forged ahead and found the correct pipeline to AAU coach, Mike Green, in Atlanta. Green informed him that to be evaluated, Ketia would have to fly there for tryouts. Certainly not an easy task, but in December, 1997, Ketia left Germany for Norcross, Georgia, for what would be the beginning of a whole new world.

Coach Green had been a little skeptical when he heard the father, of yet another ten-year-old, say, "My girl is really good." After all, he'd heard the same declaration many times from proud, but unrealistic parents who believed their daughter was the next Cheryl Miller (University of Southern California All American, Three-time College Player of the Year, and WNBA great).

Although the Georgia Magic had a decent finish in the AAU ten-under team national championship tournament the previous summer, it was clear they needed to upgrade the roster if they were going to compete with the top teams around the States. Among other things, they needed *taller players*.

Coach Green and Jim Nichols, founder and assistant coach, eagerly anticipated the December meeting with Ketia and her dad at Meadowcreek High School.

"When they walked into the gym," Nichols recalled, "we probably had a brief moment of disappointment, simply because Ketia was not the tall player we felt we desperately needed." The disappointment quickly disappeared. "I don't know if we had ever seen a young lady, her age, with that sort of speed, quickness, and ball control ability. We immediately offered her a spot on our upcoming eleven-under team."

Mike Green echoed Jim's assessment. "I fell in love with her as a player, but respected who she was on and off the court." For once, he admitted, a parent had been correct. Ketia's intense desire, work ethic, skill, and willingness to learn, were immediately recognized. "I wasn't surprised at how special she was when I met her parents. The dynamics of their extended family, made you almost envious!"

With Ketia's basketball prowess validated, she would need to demonstrate another crucial trait; teamwork.

"We preached, a very 'team oriented' style of ball. With that, you wouldn't normally see one player with dominant statistics," Nichols remarked. No need to worry about their latest recruit. Ketia's team-high 79 assists that first year proved she was no ball hog.

Another trait he discovered was her willingness to mentor those around her. "One of our favorite training exercises was to have younger teams practice with our older teams. In our club, all of the teams ran the same offense and a lot of the same drills. Ketia was never reluctant to spend time with the younger players, and was a role model for many of them."

The only one who didn't remember her generosity, on and off the court, was Ketia. While her coaches and former players praised her unselfish attitude toward the game and her teammates, she didn't see anything special about her actions. "Mentoring? I don't remember that. I may have given other players a few tips, now and then." Humility was also deeply ingrained in her character.

In order to be an official member of the team, it would be necessary to pull her out of her German school in May and fly to the States to qualify for the Georgia AAU state tournament. Getting her there would be no problem, but where would she stay? As First Sergeants, both parents had too much responsibility to take off the time required. No problem! Coming to the rescue was Ketia's Uncle Aaron (Uncle Chief as he was affectionately known) and family, in Marietta, Georgia.

After successfully qualifying for the tournament, Ketia returned briefly to Germany, where she ran wind sprints with her dad to increase her strength and resilience. Then, it was back to Georgia in June to play in the state tournament. So many long roundtrips, but everything was now in place for success. All Ketia had to do was live up to the high expectations that followed her across the Atlantic.

Another fast-approaching extended stay in the states left Smokey and Rosie nervous about leaving her, especially since it was imperative she stay close to the gym for practice and games. Enter Liz Nichols, wife of the Georgia Magic founder, backbone, and the mother figure to all the girls. If someone needed a ride, "Miss Liz" was there to provide it. If someone needed a temporary home, the Nichols' answered the call. They were delighted to take Ketia in and treat her like family. Ketia's path to success cleared another hurdle.

After a successful basketball season in America, she returned to Germany in the fall. Another year with the junior girls earned the team the *U.S. Army Europe Championship,* with Ketia receiving the Most Valuable Player Award.

Her return to Georgia the next year was a little less challenging. Ketia and her parents had not only come to terms with her being alone in another country, they were more familiar with program expectations. Ketia's needs, and ability to live as normal a life as possible, would be met by the entire AAU family.

The companionship Ketia found with her teammates was an extra bonus. "We not only played together four-plus years, we found comfort in each other outside basketball. Those girls were the one 'constant' in my life at the time I needed it most."

AAU NATIONAL BASKETBALL CHAMPIONSHIP
OVERLAND PARK, KANSAS - 2002

She also looked forward to occasional visits to the homes of teammates. "I couldn't wait for AAU season to hoop and hang out with my Georgia Magic family. I especially loved staying with the Brown family in Dalton, Georgia. Being with them was like visiting with my aunts, uncles, and cousins."

Living with a non-military family, like the Browns, also allowed a certain distance from constant worries whether her dad was safe during his second deployment to Saudi Arabia. "I did my best to spend those days concentrating on basketball, but soon discovered there was simply no way to forget, even if I wanted to."

One evening, while watching on-going reports of the war on the evening news, Mr. Brown asked about her feelings. "I casually told him I didn't get to talk to my dad too often and had no idea when, or if, I would see him again. I still remember how emotionless I sounded. Deep down, I missed my father more than words could describe, but I hid those feelings for fear the flood gates would open if I didn't."

While Ketia found comfort on a personal level with her living arrangements, Smokey saw it from a practical standpoint. "Not only were necessary expenses relieved, Ketia's commitments allowed us the opportunity to get back to the states twice a year for reunions." (Swanier reunions, complete with picnics and crab boils, were, and still are, legendary)

In late 1999, their long-distance problems appeared to be solved when the Swaniers received a compassionate reassignment due to Corena Swanier's health crisis and upcoming heart transplant. The plan, however, to transfer from Germany to Fort Benning, Georgia, was changed at the last minute to a base in California. No one wanted this move; especially Smokey and Rosie. During such a trying time, they needed to be near family in Mississippi; not clear across the country.

Ketia's coaches and teammates kicked into high gear, and organized a campaign to reverse the orders. Miss Liz got on board and, along with 300 girls, wrote letters and made phone calls to Georgia Senator, Sam Nunn, and other state officials. "You can't let these people go to California. They have to stay here; not so much for basketball, but because they are such a good family and good people." Coach Green admits the motives to keep the family local were not completely unselfish. "I wanted Ketia on my team!"

The campaign was a success! Sergeants First Class, Cornell and Rosie Swanier, were assigned to Fort Benning Army Base where Ketia began eighth grade at Arnold Middle School. Although she had to learn, once again, to "fit in" at another new school, she was thrilled to be close to her Georgia Magic teammates. Rather than traveling halfway around the world, she was now just a couple hours away from practice and actual games.

Aside from their support of Ketia, the Georgia Magic family was near and dear to Smokey's heart for another reason. Before Twitter, Instagram, and Facebook, parents had to rely on "snail mail" photos and newspaper articles of all the games and fun activities that centered on the team. Still, any news of his daughter's activities was the most precious gift Smokey received. "That was before everyone recorded videos with their phones." He laughed. "So, every package they provided was priceless."

Their support not only meant the world to him, but to his company as well. "The day I'd get those large envelopes in the desert, I couldn't wait to share the contents with my soldiers. It instantly made me feel as though we were there together enjoying Ketia and her teammates."

While one problem was solved with their move to the states, Rosie's role became more tangible in nature. More often than not, she was the one charged with driving Ketia from Columbus to Atlanta two or three times a week for practice. Having lived on military bases for the past twenty years, Rosie wasn't thrilled with driving the packed highways around Atlanta. "I'd have to pry my hands off the steering wheel after more than a few rush-hour trips."

One summer she even had to drive her daughter to Florida and back for Nationals. "Those were the times I missed my husband the most." Normally, the couple would've made plans at the dinner table to make the drive, together. "Now, I was on my own. What route/direction would be the best? What time should we get on the interstate?" There was also the added pressure to make sure Ketia had everything she needed for the trip; basketball shoes, uniforms, documents, etc. "She was the main focus, and I had to be mentally and physically prepared." It was whole new ballgame, so to speak, when it came to her child.

Despite the strain of coordinating trips and travel, mostly by Rosie while Smokey was deployed, both parents agreed it was well worth the cost, time accumulated, and every ounce of sweat that was given.

The competitive nature of AAU and the large pool of talent meant Ketia had to step up her game. Basketball had come easily for her, but she was now part of a team consisting of equally gifted players. Practice was tough, physically and mentally, but she knew playing with the Magic could be a major step toward realizing her dreams.

One episode stuck out that typified Ketia's persistence. During a game at the national tournament in 1999 in Springfield, Missouri, she was handling the ball and got trapped by two or three defenders right in front of the Magic bench.

"As only Ketia could do," Nichols recalled, "she dribbled the basketball between her legs and behind her back, doing everything in her power to prevent the ball from being stolen."

At one point, she looked at (Coach Green) Mike and pleaded, "What should I do?"

He shrugged. "You got yourself in this mess. Get yourself out."

That's exactly what the point guard did. Adding a couple of fakes and another behind-the-back dribble, she shook the defenders and drove to the basket.

Ketia's memories of hard work and basketball drills also held some light-hearted moments. "Mr. Jim promised, if we got to a certain number of victories during the season, he'd shave off his mustache," she quipped. "He'd had it for about 30 years, but, as you can guess, he became clean-shaven that summer."

2001 AAU NATIONAL CHAMPIONSHIPS - LAFAYETTE, LA

SWEET SIXTEEN - FINAL FOUR - 2ND PLACE

"Mr. Jim" remembers it well. "At the 1998 eleven-under National Tournament in Kenner, Louisiana, the team played tremendous basketball and made the 'Sweet 16', ultimately finishing 7th. The night after we won the game that insured our position, we all gathered in my room to witness the event. I still have a picture of me shaving my face, with all of the girls gathered around, laughing."

Oh, but that wasn't the end of promises he would live to regret. Not one to back off issuing challenges, he took it a step further at the fourteen-under national tournament in 2001. "I promised that if we were one of the final four teams, I'd let them braid my hair into 'corn rows'. Well, of course they did; even surpassing expectations by making it to the finals. Trust me. It was a *bad look* for someone with red, stringy hair."

Nationals were in different cities every year, such as Orlando, Knoxville, Philadelphia, and Kansas City, so the experience of visiting different cities with diverse cultures, and lifestyles throughout the country, was exciting for Ketia and her family.

Coach Green recalled one game in which nearly *one hundred* of the Swanier's relatives sat in the stands. "I looked at the bleachers and couldn't believe it!"

For the next seven years, with the eleven-under through seventeen-under teams, Ketia helped lead the Magic to seven consecutive Georgia AAU State Championships, and seven consecutive 'Sweet 16' finishes at the AAU National Championships, where, typically, over 100 teams participated.

After the team's 2004 final AAU tournament at Disney Wide World of Sports in Orlando, a group picture was snapped including players, parents, relatives, and supporters. "There were probably fifty to sixty people in the picture," Nichols claimed, "and I'm guessing, at least 75% of those were Ketia's relatives. It highlighted what a great group of team parents we had over that seven-year stretch, and nobody came out in more numbers than the Swanier clan."

That picture still hangs in his office. "Great times and great memories," he added.

Through all the flights from Europe and back, the hours spent on interstates from Columbus, Georgia to

Atlanta, and the trips to AAU tournaments, the Swaniers had faith their sacrifice, along with Ketia's talent, experience, and dedication, would, one day, pay for her college education. To support their faith, during that time she received her first visit and recruitment letter from the college coach at Auburn University.

Ketia's dreams, however, went even farther than college. Her goal, to play in the WNBA, intensified during the 2004 nationals where she had the opportunity to see her first professional game between the Orlando Miracles and the Sacramento Monarchs. "Watching those talented women play the game I loved made me more determined than ever to be drafted into the league."

Could her dreams become reality?

"I didn't want to see him go. He's been deployed before. I'm not worried about anything. I've been dealing with this my whole life. I might as well say I'm in the Army too. I just really miss him."
—**Ketia on her father leaving for Kuwait**

Chapter Four: Columbus High School

Before Ketia entered the ninth grade, her dad received call-after-call from *high school* coaches trying to recruit his daughter. "Enroll her in our school," they'd appeal. "She'll love it here and will be a guaranteed four-year starter."

It appeared, to Smokey, the family had several options to consider. What he didn't consider was that Rosie had already researched and chosen the right school for her daughter. Not only was Columbus High a sports powerhouse, it was, academically, one of the best in Georgia. While basketball was vitally important in Ketia's life, to Rosie, it was secondary to her future.

Although Ketia was happy with her new school, freshman year was not without controversy. Her basketball accomplishments had followed her from middle-school and AAU. She had a lot to live up to, and no one was going to give her a pass.

The 2001-2002 basketball season, was an unusual one in the South Georgia city. Three local schools jockeyed back and forth for honors; Columbus High, Spencer, and Shaw. The Columbus Lady Blue Devils moved into contention with wins over both their city rivals, elevating them from fifteenth in the state polls to tenth, overall.

While Ketia's intention was to adjust to high school and play basketball, one of her teammates increased the tension among the rival schools and players—especially between Columbus and Spencer—by calling freshman, Swanier, "the best player in town." *A quote that*

Ketia played for the Columbus Lady Blue Devils

was repeated in the Columbus Ledger-Enquirer. According to Ketia's teammate, she was even better than the 2000 Ledger-Enquirer girls' basketball player of the year, Nikita Bell, who was headed to the University of North Carolina that fall. The Spencer coach dismissed the comment, but it drove the rivalry, none-the-less.

Both players lived up to their reputations. The freshman, Swanier, averaged 12 Points, 5 Rebounds, 6 Assists, 5 Steals per game, and was selected to the Atlanta Tip-Off Club Georgia High School Association AAAA All Region Team of the Year. Bell, a senior, was named Miss Georgia Basketball and Class AAAA player of the year.

Ketia credits her years at Columbus High School as the turning point of her basketball future, especially during her freshman year. "Playing against really good players as a freshman, made me realize I had a little bit of game in me, and that basketball could be a part of my future." Yes, the Columbus High School guard definitely had game.

While Ketia adjusted to the added pressures of homework and basketball, she began her sophomore year with more confidence and less stress on the basketball court. The year ended, however, with an event the family knew was possible, but were never truly prepared to face; her dad's deployment orders.

Early one morning, Rosie drove Smokey to Fort Benning for his imminent departure to Kuwait during Operation Desert Spring, 2002. Ketia, scared and heartbroken, chose to stay home rather than watch him leave from the airport. "I knew I'd cry and didn't want to make it any more difficult on him and my mom."

Smokey also remembers how hard it was to say goodbye. "The weekend before I left for the Middle East, Rosie and I attended Ketia's track event at Columbus

High. Sitting in the bleachers watching my girl compete, I realized it would be the last sporting event I would see for a long while. It was hard to imagine leaving in the middle of her being highly recruited by colleges and universities, along with missing her entire second summer season with the Georgia Magic."

It would be tough for all three Swaniers. Rosie had the role of sole parent, and Ketia would, once again, have to make-do without her dad's daily encouragement and support. Smokey would, once again have to make-do with less-than-satisfying audio tapes and newspaper accounts in order to keep in touch with Ketia's practices and games.

Mother and daughter responsibilities for running the home were not easy since Rosie had professional duties of her own. As the First Sergeant in charge of Bravo Company with 30th AG Battalion, she had to leave before day break to check the barracks, make formation for Physical Training (P.T.) exercise, and then go back home to take Ketia to school. Time was crucial, and Rosie knew that one slip could easily throw off the daily schedule. Ketia would have to be responsible and reliable; not just some days, but every day. Most mornings, she was up to the challenge. By the time Rosie would return home, her daughter had made her own breakfast, finished eating, and was waiting for her ride to school.

As with most teens, Ketia was eager to get her driver's license and the freedom it allowed. That freedom, however, was crucial to Rosie, as well. If Ketia could drive, Rosie would no longer have to leave work in order to meet her daughter's hectic schedule.

Anticipating the need, Smokey had just begun to teach his daughter to drive a stick shift when he had to deploy. Rosie would be required to finish the training.

Fortunately, by the time she took over, Ketia had the fundamentals down but still needed lots of practice. "More so than Dad, Mom forced me to be independent. Dad kind of babied me along, but Mom would say, 'Ketia, just get in the car and drive.'"

In the beginning, Ketia wasn't too sure about driving on her own, but Rosie assured her she *could* and *would* learn to drive a standard shift. She practiced, practiced, and practiced until she got it. "That was a huge load off of me," Rosie admitted. "I was so proud that she never said she couldn't do it. She smiled and kept trying until it came naturally to her. I just knew, as a mother always knows, what my child is capable of doing."

As was usually the case, both her parents had worked in perfect unison; giving their daughter the skills to inspire the confidence she'd use throughout life.

Most days seemed pretty ordinary for Rosie and Ketia while Smokey was gone. One incident in the spring of 2003, however, shook their feelings of security to the core.

Behind Ketia's school was a large dirt area for student parking. The space where she usually parked was often blocked in by other cars, so it would always take a few extra minutes before she could leave. That particular day, going about her normal routine, she threw her book bag in the car, but decided to talk with some friends while traffic cleared. Along with the independence, Ketia felt good being able to drive to school and practices; allowing her mother time away from chauffeur duties. As to the freedom it allowed, she appreciated spending a little extra time catching up on school gossip.

After sharing a few laughs with friends, she took the usual route home. She pulled into the family driveway, entered the house, and went straight to her room, as was her daily habit. Being familiar with every square inch and every personal item, she noticed, immediately, her PlayStation was missing. As a typical teenager, her first thought was that her mother had taken away her favorite game because she'd gotten home a little late the day before. Nothing else was missing in the room or looked out of place, so she shrugged it off.

Without the temptation of playing her favorite game, she dove into her homework; unaware of the moment Rosie arrived home until she heard her mom scream, *"Ketia! Ketia!* Where are you?" It was no ordinary day.

Ketia ran from her bedroom. "What? What's going on?"

Her mother stood, wide-eyed, panicked. "How did you not see this?"

It was only then Ketia noticed the sunroom window; shattered glass sprayed across the floor.

"Someone broke in. Are you sure you're okay?" Rosie asked. By that time, Ketia had processed the scene before her and realized Rosie wasn't upset at her, but frightened for her and what could've happened had she been present during the home invasion. Being a single parent was stressful enough. Add to that, the strain of knowing your home was no longer a safe haven. Rosie's peace of mind had been violated, as had Ketia's.

Within the hour, the police came and dusted for prints. Footprints determined there had been two burglars and, from the items that were taken, along with those left behind, police suspected the house had been targeted. It was clear the thieves knew the best place to enter and what to look for. The selected items taken were never recovered, and those responsible were never caught, but the loss of "tangibles" was secondary to the emotional toll. It would be a long time before Mother and Daughter felt secure in the home; especially during the months Smokey was deployed.

"When I think back to this story, I have a new appreciation for what my mother went through. Single mom responsibilities, stressing about Dad's safety; I don't know, to this day, how she dealt with the break-in without falling apart. On top of that," Ketia added, she never missed one of my games."

After the break-in, Ketia was eager to return to the relative normalcy of school and sports.

As Ketia moved toward the end of her second season on the high school basketball team, the University of Connecticut Women's Huskies were winning a national championship in Atlanta —not far from her Georgia home.

Smokey Swanier was halfway around the world. The U.S. Army's 3rd Infantry, making up Swanier and his 216 troops, were in Baghdad during the height of Operation Iraqi Freedom.

The images of the toppling statue of Saddam Hussein were broadcast across the globe, highlighting the success of Swanier's mission. But a different set of images, sent from Columbus to Iraq, were the ones Smokey treasured the most.

Packages filled with news clips and videos of his daughter kept the First Sergeant going. "Tapes of her games; always keeping me informed about what was going on with her, made the stress of war a little easier."

After sharing Ketia's exploits with his soldiers, they, in turn, adopted her as their favorite player, and followed her progress right along with her proud father. "She had a big, strong support system with the troops," Smokey said. "They always talked about her, because they knew her father, and because she was so good. Ketia was not only special to them, they supported her through me. They knew there was nothing I wanted more than to get home in time to see Columbus High make that year's Georgia state championship run. That was the type of cohesive unit we had. We all stuck together."

Ketia earned many honors while playing high school basketball. She was three-time Georgia AAAA All-State First Team, three-time All Bi-City Player of the Year, and Georgia AAAA Player of the Year her senior year.

Her experiences at Columbus High were valuable, not only for the chance to play with, and against, the best competition, but, academically, she had survived and thrived at one of the best schools in Georgia. Ketia, however, was blissfully unaware of the challenges she would face the moment she entered college. Not only would her course schedule be brutal, her physical, mental, and emotional endurance would be tested to the max.

Columbus High retired Ketia's jersey, along with honoring her success at UConn and in the WNBA

I have my priorities set and I am content looking forward to attaining my goals.

—*Military Brat*

Chapter Five: College Recruitment

After receiving Georgia First team All-State awards at Columbus High, it was time to nail down a college. The Swaniers devoted the same amount of dedication and precision to this process as they did everything else in their lives.

The first task, for Ketia, was to shrink her list to fifteen colleges and universities. Once this was accomplished, Smokey got involved in the process by making phone calls to head coaches from her selected schools. The first question, and most relevant on his mind; "Do you have an immediate place in your starting lineup for Ketia?" If the answer was, "No", he'd press on. "Would you offer her a scholarship, today?" The conversation ended politely if the answer was also negative, which very few were. Most schools and coaches were so enthusiastic towards the high school star's ability they had already begun the recruiting process when she was in eighth grade.

The pros and cons of each college were very carefully weighed, ten programs were eliminated, and Ketia's top five "wish list" remained: University of Connecticut, Georgia Tech, Virginia Tech, Old Dominion, and Clemson.

The University of Georgia didn't recruit Ketia, but the Swaniers still decided to take advantage of an invitation to visit the campus and get familiar with the basketball program. The Lady Bulldogs were loaded with guards that season and the Georgia coach admitted that 5'5" Ketia might ride the bench for a couple of years. But, as it turned out, Coach Landers still played a vital role in the school that *would* offer Ketia a coveted scholarship. He suggested she could play, immediately, at UConn. In fact, he admitted she could play almost anywhere. Her skills were solid and she was coachable; two factors that weighed heavily when it came to offering scholarships. Landers made a phone call and, within three weeks, head coach, Coach Geno Auriemma, confirmed arrangements to visit Columbus to watch Ketia practice.

Georgia Magic coach, Mike Green made himself available to pick up the coach at the airport and take him to watch Ketia practice. Little was discussed about her on the way to the gym, but Green was confidant her talent and persistence would speak for itself.

Auriemma sat quietly watching the senior, along with the team, complete practice drills before asking a few questions about Ketia's family life and her overall attitude. Hearing a glowing, yet honest, report from Green, the UConn coach agreed. "She's a keeper. She's fast enough, but is she tall enough?" Mike, who'd had the pleasure of coaching Ketia for years, compared her to Spud Webb, former NBA player. "In 1982," he informed the Huskie coach, "Webb led the Midland, Texas Chaparrals to the junior college national title in 1982. The 5'7" Webb led all scorers with 36 points, making 10 of 15 shots from the floor and 16 of 18 from the free-throw line." That tournament performance earned him a write-up in *Sports Illustrated*, along with national attention. "She can do everything Webb can do," Green stated, unequivocally.

Green's observations didn't stop with the UConn coach. He also raved about Swanier's skills to the *Hartford Courant*. "She's a superior ball handler and one of the fastest girls you're ever going to find. She's going to be extremely entertaining. She's a wizard with the basketball."

Coach Auriemma soon discovered the truth in Green's words. Ketia became the first freshman, since Sue Bird in 1998, to open the season as the starting guard. A surprise to no one who knew her strengths, she was touted as, possibly, the fastest player to ever put on a Huskie uniform. Even Auriemma called her the fastest player in the history of the program.

Green had been around long enough, however, to know the huge leap Ketia would face from high school to college ball, but he still had complete faith in her natural ability and basketball I.Q.

"I think when Geno came down here and explained to her that when you come to Connecticut you have to have the guts to put a bull's-eye on your back, that's who Ketia is," Green assured. "She doesn't want it easy. She wants to earn it and she wants to be the best there is. That's the way she practices. That's the way she thinks. That's the way her mom and dad have brought her up, that's the girl that has been in my program, and that's what she gave the last six years she played with us." Green went on to say, "She's one of the most honorable, respectful kids you'll find." He discovered that fact on a personal level in 2009 during Breast Cancer Awareness Month when Ketia, who then played for the WNBA Phoenix Mercury, sent a jersey to Mike's wife who was battling breast cancer. "She never failed to send birthday and Christmas cards, either."

Before Auriemma left Columbus that day, he expressed a strong desire to add Ketia to Connecticut's roster, not only because of her talents, but to have the opportunity to include her parents in the program. "I wish every set of parents of recruits would be like the Swaniers."

The Huskie coach admired the twenty-year commitment Smokey and Rosie Swanier made to their country; the responsibility and sacrifices made when leaving Ketia during deployments. He noted the couple showed no bitterness about putting themselves in the line of fire. "You don't find that every day."

While Ketia loved the recruiting process and fell in love with UConn and the program, true to her empathetic nature, she had a hard time notifying the other colleges of the decision. "They had spent years building a relationship, and I hated to disappoint them. They all had great programs. Just not for me."

Ketia Committed to UConn

During her October 2003 visit to UConn, Ketia conveyed her impressions of the campus and the program. "I liked the intensity on the floor, the coaching style. Everybody gives 100 percent. I like the way the players talk. I like all that stuff. It looks like they have fun together. Why would you want to go somewhere where they don't get along?"

I've been trained, since day one, to endure the changing winds of life and to make the best of what is given to me.

— Military Brat

Chapter Six: UConn:

If the freshman had one flaw during her years playing competitive sports, especially when it came to basketball, it was her quiet demeanor. To get her to step up and assume a leadership role was challenging throughout her career. "When you're part of a team, you need to use your skills to make that team perform at the highest level," Coach Green noted. Her years with the Huskies, and their demanding coach, helped Ketia overcome her natural tendency to go quietly about her business, on and off the court.

Freshman year is difficult for anyone, but it was even more grueling than Ketia expected. The transition from high school to college classes, along with the rigors of basketball, practice, and the rise in competition, tested her positive attitude. She was determined, however, to make the most of her opportunity. She also knew her mom would be checking on her grades. *Added stress!*

Rosie, however, struggled with stress of her own as a mother whose child was beginning the first year of college. Student athletes are required to enroll several months in advance in order to settle in and begin conditioning exercises. Smokey couldn't make the trip to Connecticut the summer of 2004 because he was in Mississippi helping care for his critically ill mother, along with celebrating his mother and dad's Fiftieth wedding anniversary. A bittersweet visit, indeed. Rosie and Ketia would have to make the trip, alone.

UConn 2008 Final Four

Rosie packed everything but the "kitchen sink" to make Ketia feel at home in her dorm room, and then stayed on campus for two more weeks getting Ketia settled. But, too soon, it was time to leave. Unable to hold back tears, she gave her daughter one final hug before heading back home to Georgia.

She cried alone in the car on the trip back; wondering if she had given Ketia the right tools to survive and cope. As with most mothers in that situation, she questioned her parenting skills. "Did I show her all the kindness and love that I had? She was so far away from home, but my heart and soul knew I had to let her go so she could achieve her goals. I was only used as a vessel. God had her in the palm of his hand." Rosie had faith that everything was in place for her daughter's success.

Ketia, preparing for her first full year at UConn as a college freshman and highly-touted basketball recruit, was kept on her toes facing a whole new set of challenges. "I didn't cry," she said of being in a strange city, different state, and new school. "I had so many emotions being away from home on my own for the first time."

College courses and high expectations of playing at one of the best women's collegiate basketball programs, ever, weighed heavily on the young athlete. UConn had not only won three NCAA championships in a row. The previous season the Huskies lost one of the best basketball players to ever play the game. High expectations were put on the incoming group, and being looked upon as a highly-regarded player from one of the best basketball schools in Georgia, Ketia felt added pressure.

The year for the Huskies started out being described as "life without Diana." *Diana Taurasi* left behind a formidable legacy. She became UConn's first two-time national player of the year in 2004 and guided the Huskies to three consecutive national championships. UConn boasted an overall mark of 139-8 during Taurasi's tenure. She was a three-time Kodak All-America selection, two-time Associated Press First Team All-America choice, and the first player in UConn history to total 2,000 points, 600 assists and 600 rebounds in a career.

Statistics aside, as leader of the team, Taurasi's fiery presence in practice and calming influence in games would be sorely missed. The incoming freshmen, including Ketia, had huge basketball sneakers to fill.

After a slow start, Ketia's speed, energy, and determination impressed the coach enough that she stepped into the point guard position in the second exhibition game. Her progress, from the first practice until the beginning of the season, was greater than anyone else on the team, Auriemma observed. She had developed the ability to change speeds on a dime. During that game, she scored five points, had two assists, and only three turnovers in twenty-two minutes of play.

Her steady performance allowed her to look forward, with anticipation, to the first regular season game against Buffalo. Even more exciting was that her dad would be in attendance. Rosie would join him for the game in North Carolina the following Sunday. The two people most responsible for Ketia's chance to play, on such a huge basketball stage, would finally have the reward of seeing their daughter fulfill her dreams.

Ketia and Grandma Corena

The "highs", however, would be balanced by incredible "lows" that year. It was probably a good thing Ketia didn't have access to a crystal ball early in the season, because the mental and emotional anguish that waited, beyond the world of Huskie basketball, would've crushed a weaker spirit. "I don't recall getting the phone call about Grandma. It's nowhere to be found in my memory. I do remember her passing away on my father's birthday, October 10, 2004." It would be Ketia's first funeral. She didn't want to go. Corena Swanier had played a major role in her upbringing. During the times Ketia stayed with her, she remembered her grandmother preaching, "Go to school. Don't worry about the boys."

Corena's death was an impossible pill for Ketia to swallow. "I crawled like a turtle up the stairs to the front church entrance. The doors were open. Right before I reached the door, my shoes, mysteriously, turned into huge cement blocks. I froze. Not being able to move my feet I leaned my body forward just past the door to peek inside. My eyes made contact with my grandmother lying peacefully in her casket. I leaned back, still unable to move. I tried with everything I had to hold back tears. I wouldn't have the chance to say, 'See you later, Grandma.' This would be my final goodbye."

Smokey remembered a conversation he had with his mother about Ketia the day before she passed. "'Tell her to shoot the ball,' she'd ordered. Those two really had a special bond. Ketia wanted her grandmother to see her play in college. It didn't happen, but we knew she'd be at all the games from then on, as Ketia's guardian angel."

Ketia adopted a ritual at the free throw line. Three dribbles before each shot, each one signifying a word: I (bounce) Love (bounce) Grandma (bounce).

After her quick trip to Mississippi for the funeral, she returned to UConn for classes and 7:00 am practices; the hardest basketball practices, physically and mentally, she'd endured in her eighteen years of life. "I had a lot to learn."

The 2004 season began with a promising win against an out-manned Buffalo team. Ketia's debut was close to perfect with eight assists and no turnovers. The following game with North Carolina was a different story, however, with the Huskies losing 71-65 in the Jimmy V Classic. Adding injury to insult, an elbow by one of her own teammates resulted in a concussion.

"I passed the ball to Jess when she flashed to the high post. I turned to rub off her for a hand off but, right before I reached her, she pivoted toward the basket, simultaneously bringing the ball back to protect it from her defender. Instead of running into a hand off or non-hand off, her elbow made instant contact with my forehead; right between the eyes. My immediate thought was that I'd transformed into a human unicorn!" The last thing she remembered was the shocked looks on the faces of her teammates when she got to the bench. That injury left her with a large knot on her head, a concussion, and two black eyes.

During Ketia's second big opportunity as a starter and first against a nationally-ranked opponent, she handled the pressure pretty well in the first half. The injury, however, meant she'd have to miss the entire second half. It was during that time the Huskies fell apart, saw a 10-point lead fade in the final five minutes, and lost 71-65.

"I don't remember much about that game." As it turned out, the rest of the team wished they could've forgotten it, too.

The game, broadcast by ESPN, was also Ketia's first experience playing before a national TV audience. It was also her first time playing against an old Georgia high school rival, Nakita Bell. The senior, Bell, bested the freshman guard by scoring 10 points to Ketia's 3, and adding 3 rebounds. Nakita, however, fouled out of the game.

The team struggled the rest of the season. After Ketia's injury and a week's worth of missed practices, she spent more time warming the bench than playing in the games. Four times she played less than ten minutes per game, including a season-low two minutes against

Colorado in December. Ketia, however, wasn't the only one in the dog house. As she struggled to regain her confidence, a career-high ten points, seven assists, three steals, and no turnovers in twenty-one minutes against Providence in early January, showed her coaches and teammates the flashes of brilliance they'd expected since her first days at UConn.

Coach Auriemma yells instructions to Ketia

An earlier phone call with her dad, during that low period, was no coincidence. "It was one of those Ketia-Smokey conversations," she acknowledged. "He told me to focus. He prepped me. He was just the person I needed to talk to."

Still, Auriemma wasn't happy with any of his freshmen.

Practice was grueling, as Ketia recalled, and the coach was ruthless. It wasn't enough to make the girls scrimmage against male players; they also had to spot their opponents 30 points! Auriemma would give the young team about three minutes to make up the difference. He was not happy when they didn't. A defensive practice he liked to utilize by including the male players was a ten-on-five zone drill. "After you've played defense against ten players, five seems like a breeze," Ketia admitted. She knew why the coach was so tough on them. With UConn's reputation, the team had a target on its back. Preparation was everything.

With only three games left in the 2004-2005 season, Ketia and Mel Thomas were given an ultimatum by the coach. "You're going to be on the bench the rest of the year unless you show me these next three games what you can do." The initial response was positive. UConn beat Pittsburgh 97-49. Swanier and Thomas answered the call with 8-11 shooting. Ketia's speed sparked a transition game that resulted in 21 fast-break points. "You look at what (Ketia) did (Tuesday) and you say if we could get that from her every night, we're a different team," Auriemma told the *New Haven Register's Karen Tucker*.

Congratulations on a well-played game

I wish every student at my university was able to have the life experience I did to prepare for this challenge.

— Military Brat

Chapter Seven: NCAAW Tournament

Preparing for the first game in the National Collegiate Athletic Association Women (NCAAW) Tournament, the coach wasn't sure what to expect when the freshman guard took the court for her first experience in post-season play. Freshmen practices had been an experience; and not a good one. Bad things seemed to happen. Assignments were missed, turnovers, frequent, and shooting was inconsistent. All that changed in their first game against Dartmouth. There they were, the three freshmen on the floor at the same time functioning like a poised, experienced unit. "I'm not going to tell you I thought Ketia was going to come out and play with all that confidence, so that was a pleasant surprise," the coach said. In the scheme of things, I guess a back-handed compliment is better than none at all. Ketia finished with seven assists and two steals.

Even though the Huskies made it to the NCAA Sweet Sixteen that year, UConn would struggle following Taurasi's graduation. They lost eight games in 2005 and failed to win the Big East regular season crown for the first time since 1993.

After her grandma passed away, Ketia made it a point to stay in touch with her grandfather. "I called him quite often on his cell phone to check on him and chat." No matter what stress and strain she'd encountered that day, talking to him always made her happy. *Papoo*, as he was known by all his grandchildren, was able to see her first five college games. Ketia even had the chance to take him to a men's game; UConn vs Villanova. She treasured those times with him, especially after losing her grandmother.

Three-year-old Ketia with her beloved Papoo

After a tough first season and school year, Ketia, and some of her teammates, were at Six Flags in late summer getting much-needed rest and relaxation when her mom called. In discovering Ketia was with friends, Rosie calmly suggested, "Okay. Call me when you can." Ketia asked if everything was okay. Rosie assured her everything was fine, but deep down, she knew something wasn't right. As soon as she got back to her dorm room, she called home and heard the terrible news. Less than a year after her grandmother's death, she'd have one last chance to say goodbye to *Papoo*.

As much as she hated funerals, she would have to experience another one in less than 10 months. Her beloved grandfather died suddenly at the age of 74. Ketia was inconsolable. Adrian Swanier had been her rock. Whenever she needed to talk about life in general, he was the one she'd turn to.

Earlier that summer, Adrian had made a special trip to Georgia, to visit Ketia. "I'll never forget it," Smokey recalled. "He phoned early on a Sunday morning and insisted, 'I want to make sure to see Ketia. I want to see Ketia before she goes back to school.'" He got his wish.

"He had an opportunity to spend a couple of hours with her. It was like he knew something. He knew he was going to pass. You go back and think about the things he did and the way he did them; it was like he knew."

Adrian Swanier was born in 1930 and served in the military before earning his master's degree from Bradley University in Peoria, Ill. In 1963, he returned to his hometown, Pass Christian, Mississippi, to teach at Randolph High School after turning down a job at Texas Southern University in Houston. Starting as a shop teacher, he eventually became the school principal, a title he held until his retirement in 1993. Active in his local church, Adrian also served on the board of directors of the local credit union. In fact, Ketia's grandfather was so revered, that when he died, his casket was carried, by foot, from the church to the cemetery. People from all over the community of 6,500 joined in the *relay for Adrian's Swanier's coffin.*

The week before his death, on July 30, 2005, and just nine months after the death of his beloved Corena, he spoke to a friend about a feeling that something *extraordinary* was on its way. "I don't know how much, but really soon we're going to get a bunch of water." The next month, on August 30, Hurricane Katrina made landfall in Bay St. Louis, Mississippi, a few miles west of the Swanier's Pass Christian home. Residents of the town still talk about his timely prophecy.

Other family members fared no better during and after the storm. Ketia's aunt, Daphne Swanier-Delaine, who lived in New Orleans, left her home in the seventh ward in New Orleans to seek shelter with her son in Baton Rouge before Katrina arrived. "It was hard to talk to the outside world to let them know what was going on and to let them know everyone was OK," she said. "My son and I slept in the back of his SUV several nights. My husband returned from overseas on Oct. 7, and we went to see our home for the first time on Oct. 8. "'Everything was covered with mud. If you touched a wall, the sheetrock crumbled. We had close to four feet of water sitting in our home for about three weeks."

Two doors down was the family-owned grocery store, bought and rebuilt by Adrian and one of his brothers decades ago and still operated by Smokey's cousin, Violet. It also sustained massive damage.

In 1969, when Smokey was seven, Hurricane Camille, a rare Category 5 storm, had only knocked some shingles off the roof. This time, the roof of the family home was completely destroyed. The carport collapsed. Rooms were flooded and ruined. After the storm, Smokey drove from Villa Rica, Georgia, his and Rosie's current home, to Mississippi to access the damage. While serving in the U.S. Army's 3rd Infantry in Iraq, shattered neighborhoods, destroyed power grids, and helicopters flying overhead were a daily occurrence. Smokey now faced the same helicopter surveillance and destruction in his beloved hometown, thousands of miles from that Middle East desert.

Still in the throes of grief over her grandfather's death, while preparing for her sophomore year at UConn, Ketia had no idea the extent of the damage to the family home. It wasn't until her dad sent pictures of the house in Pass Christian via cellphone that the personal horror of Katrina revealed itself.

"Everything was gone," Ketia said. "The streets were all underwater. The storm picked up cars and threw them back onto the ground." She couldn't believe it was the same place she'd visited a few months earlier.

Factored into a difficult preseason was now the extended period of mourning for her grandfather along with mourning the complete devastation of the family's hometown.

Although Coach Auriemma was busy getting the team ready for the upcoming year, he understood his young player's difficulty in getting back to work. She had so many things happen; her grandmother, her grandfather both dying within a short period of time of each other. Piling on was the hurricane. Auriemma knew Ketia was quiet and sensitive to begin with. Any one of those events might be enough to send her crawling into a shell. He was right. The losses, combined with the storm devastation, sent her into a tailspin.

But if it is true that her grandfather predicted Katrina, and even his own death, perhaps Ketia could draw strength from one of his final conversations with her dad.

Smokey and Rosie had spent many nights pacing; worrying about their daughter from a thousand miles away. But Adrian had made one last prediction before he died that would ease their minds. During a conversation with Smokey, on his last visit, he'd said, "Ketia's going to be fine. She's going to have a really good year. She's going to be fine." He'd been accurate in his prediction about Katrina, so who would question his faith in Ketia?

After that first tough year as a team, the Lady Huskies went to the Elite Eight the following two years. The guard play improved with Renee Montgomery, Mel Thomas, and Ketia, and was bolstered with the addition of #1 ranked high school player in the country, Tina Charles. UConn, once again, emerged as a contender in 2007. The Huskies were a #1 seed in the tournament but would fall in the regional final to LSU to end the season at 32–4.

After a bitter recruitment battle with Tennessee, the 2007-2008 brought the addition of a second #1 recruit, Maya Moore. The team went through the season with only one loss; two points to Rutgers. They avenged that loss in the NCAA tournament, but eventually fell to Stanford in the semi-finals ending their season 32-2.

Although her four years never brought a coveted national championship, Ketia considers her time at UConn, under the wing of Coach Auriemma, invaluable, not only in her sports growth, but in life experience, as well. In Ketia's own words, "He's a perfectionist, anything less he won't accept. He knows what each player is capable of doing, and is hard on you if you're not meeting his expectations."

She went on to acknowledge, "I struggled tremendously my first few years. I never quit. Each year I improved. Even if it was baby steps, I improved." She had tremendous support from the guard coach, Tonya Cardoza, currently the head coach at Temple University, who saw Ketia's potential and never gave up on her. "Her support helped me become a better basketball player and make it through those rigorous college years."

She spent her final year at UConn coming off the bench, but one of her favorite memories, in college was against DePaul University. Down seventeen points with just over fifteen minutes to play, the Huskies battled back. With the score 76-75, in favor of DePaul, forward, Maya Moore, stole the ball. UConn had one last chance with 7.2 seconds to play, in the final regular season game, to take sole possession in the Big East Conference.

Coach Auriemma drew up a play. "You're going to make the winning shot," he told Ketia. The ball thrown into the speedy guard, she drove down the floor. The DePaul player guarding her moved off. Number 11 saw an opening, sped to the basket, and scored with 1.4 seconds remaining. "Tina [Charles] set a screen for me. The player guarding me shifted to another UConn player leaving an opening to the basket. I looked up, saw the lane, and raced to the basket." The Huskies won, 77-76.

Winning shot against DePaul

Thanks to a 66-56 win over Rutgers in the 2008 Greensboro Regional, the Huskies were in the final four for the first time since 2004. Thanks, in no small part, to Ketia Swanier who scored 15 points in the come-from-behind victory.

And while Georgia teammate, Maya Moore, was chosen Most Outstanding Player after the regional victory, both Moore and Renee Montgomery saw that choice differently. "Ketia was the MVP," Montgomery said after the game. "She did a great job running the offense and did a great job guarding Matee Ajavon (Rutgers guard), and that's hard to do. And she did it for 40 minutes. She was definitely the best player." Moore also agreed the award should've gone to Swanier.

Along with UConn going to the final four, Ketia won the inaugural *Big East Sixth Man of the Year Award* as a senior coming off the bench. She was the only UConn player in program history to rank among the top ten career leaders in games played (142), assists (479), and steals (247).

Throughout her four years playing for the Huskies, her dad only missed four games. *Four games in four years!* That feat would be a hardship for any parent under *normal* circumstances. Traveling from Georgia, to almost every game the Big East team played, was a logistics nightmare in itself. Add to that, an Army veteran with severe PTSD, especially when it came to loud noises and crowds, and the battle was almost insurmountable. Smokey persisted, however, and credits those games with giving him a reason to move forward and get back to living. To this day he says, "Ketia made the world go around for us." She most certainly made the world a less intimidating place for her dad to begin repairing the emotional and physical damage that war and constant deployment had generated.

Not to be outdone in the "dedicated parent department" was Rosie. She attended almost as many games as Ketia's dad, but her focus remained on her daughter's full college experience; education first, basketball, second. Rosie's role was different but equal to Smokey's. While he focused on Ketia's basketball training and attitude, she was all about seeing that her daughter would have the tools to make it in a world *without* basketball. Make no mistake. Rosie's love of basketball; playing and watching, was every bit as strong, but she wanted her daughter prepared for whatever life had in store.

In the spring of 2008, Ketia's days at UConn were coming to an end. "During graduation ceremonies, I know Grandma and Papoo were looking down with smiles covering their faces." Looking on, with equally proud smiles, were Smokey and Rosie.

All that hard work and dedication had paid off. Ketia, a sociology major, was determined to use her degree to further her own career and help other military brats discover their own paths.

Senior night – Proud parents
Rosie, Coach Auriemma , Ketia, Smokey

Every day brings a new opportunity to learn life-changing lessons

– Military Brat

Chapter Eight: Playing in the WNBA

When one door closes, another opens.

In 2008, Ketia was drafted in the first round (12th) by the Connecticut Sun. She played in 25 of 34 possible games, with 6 starts and ranked 14th in the league in steals per 40 minutes (2.24). That wasn't enough to keep her from being waived by the Sun because of the 11-woman roster cuts the following year.

After being told she needed to play overseas to get more experience, getting waived was another door that appeared to close. Immediately after learning of her dismissal during a meeting with Sun's head coach, Mike Thibault, and assistant coach, Bernadette Mattox, she called her dad. She choked out the news she'd received through a "rainstorm of tears". Needless to say, his daughter's heartbreak ended that day's golf game for Smokey. "Thank goodness he was close by in Connecticut at the time," she recalled.

They packed that same day, loaded her car with her belongings and drove back to Georgia. With the heartbreak still fresh in her mind, she did some pretty heavy self-talking on the way home. "It is what it is. God has a plan for me. Everything happens for a reason. I decided to just keep working hard, keep my head up and continue to move forward." Smokey and Rosie expected no less of their daughter and knew she'd be okay.

Ketia had almost no time to wonder if, or when, that next door would open. The day after she got home, her agent, at the time, contacted her about the Phoenix Mercury wanting to add her to their roster. "I gave her a 'yes' without any hesitation, even though I had to *unpack* to *repack* to get on a flight to Arizona the next day."

Diana Taurasi shares a teaching moment during the championship run

After a whirlwind flight to Phoenix, she retrieved her luggage from baggage claim and went outside into what could only be described as a sauna. She only *thought* Georgia was hot in the summer. Phoenix gave her a taste of how it felt to be biscuits baking inside an oven.

Heat aside, she joined the Mercury on June 3, 2009. The following October, the Phoenix Mercury defeated the Indiana Fever 94-86 in Game 5 to claim their second WNBA championship.

2008 WNBA Champions – The Phoenix Mercury, Ketia sitting 1st row on right

From the early blog on Ketia4Kidz:

October 13, 2009 - On October 9, 2009, Ketia Swanier and the Phoenix Mercury defeated the Indiana Fever for the 2009 WNBA Championship. A proven winner, Ketia now adds WNBA champion to her impressive resume. The former Georgia AAAA Player of the Year and UCONN standout played a key role throughout the season and playoffs, backing up Temeka Johnson at the point guard position. Having started the season with the Connecticut Sun, Ms. Swanier quickly adapted to the new up-tempo pace of the Phoenix Mercury *providing quickness, defensive pressure and leadership for the Mercury.*

This season was a dream-come-true for the 2nd year player out of UCONN. Players such as Johnson and Diana Taurasi spoke throughout the season about the spark that Ketia provided off of the bench. Ms. Swanier credited Johnson for making the transition easier in the new system and on a new team. The future is promising for the guard, as she will be asked to perform at an even higher level for the Mercury, while pressing the defense with her penetration and improved jump shot.

The thrill of winning a championship led to another life-changing moment in Ketia's life. Since she didn't experience the joy of a national championship at UConn, a trip to the White House honoring the Mercury's WNBA championship, was a dream come true.

In Ketia's own words: "Today I had an experience of a lifetime! I joined my WNBA teammates for our visit to the White House to meet President Obama for winning the 2009 WNBA Championship! You have no idea how great this felt. I stood behind the President when he honored us, and then stood next to him for our team picture! Not often am I star struck, but meeting the President of the United States is one of those moments that you're never really prepared for! You might think you have the words to say, but when you meet President Obama, it all goes out of the window!

I was hoping to meet our First Lady, Michelle Obama, as I'm a huge fan of hers and what she's doing for military families and children. We're making plans to find a way to work with her.

Visit to White House. Ketia standing to the left of President Barack Obama

Let's Move (another First Lady initiative to fight childhood obesity), and Ketia4Kidz (my charity which benefits military families) combine to bring more to our military children.

It began with my teammates and I putting on a basketball clinic at the White House for our youth. It was really hot, but we all enjoyed it. Giving back is what I'm about, so this was the perfect way to end our White House visit. The kids were active, and we were able to take pictures, share experiences and bring smiles to their faces.

Basketball clinic at the White House

More than that, though, I'm motivated to win it all again and make it back to the White House! In the meantime, I'll keep working on my game, and then working to make a difference for our military children! Thanks for everyone's support!"

While her three years with the Mercury were uneven, on one particular night, in July, 2010, her fighting spirit took over when she watched a teammate take a blow from the opposition. She was suspended one game by the WNBA during an altercation in the Mercury's Saturday night game against the New York Liberty. Never one to instigate a fight, Ketia, nevertheless, left the bench and confronted New York's Cappie Pondexter who had smacked the Mercury's Penny Taylor in the face. The diminutive Mercury guard was ejected, and would miss the game at Los Angeles the following Tuesday night.

Anyone who believes basketball isn't a contact sport, needs to rethink that position.

A year later, Ketia was on the receiving end of what could have been a frightening injury. She went down in a heap late in the third quarter after taking an elbow to the left eye from Sparks guard Kristi Toliver, who swung her arm while trying to protect the ball. Ketia was carried from the game, her eye swollen shut.

Another chapter closed when she was waived by the Sun in 2012. But the dream didn't end. Not for this military brat who grew up knowing the future was not guaranteed; that the only certainty in life is uncertainty. Her free agency status allowed her to join the Atlanta Dream and sign a multi-year contract. Marynell Meadors, a former assistant on Geno Auriemma's Olympic Gold Medal winning team in 2012, was the Dream coach. While many considered the opportunity the chance to "come home", for the former Georgia standout, Ketia viewed it as strictly business.

Ketia, and her former UConn teammate, guard, Tiffany Hayes, each in her first season in Atlanta, came off the bench for the two-time defending Eastern Conference champions during playoffs in 2012 against the Indiana Fever. Unfortunately, Coach Meadors was dismissed from the team because of a conflict with the WNBA's leading scorer, the Dream's Angel McCoughtry.

"Yes, we had a lot of ups and downs that season," Ketia admitted. "But we made the playoffs and got our act together." The big thing was they played through adversity. She hadn't been home for an extended period of time since high school. But that's what a military brat learns to do. "You're resilient. You learn how to adjust to things."

"It was nice having my parents get to see me play, but they don't live in the same town I grew up in. And like most everyone who goes away to college, and moves around the country, there's a sense of disconnect with some of the people you knew when you were growing up. Still, being closer to home was great, for professional and personal reasons.

Swanier appeared in all 34 games for the Dream, averaging 11.4 minutes with two starts. But her playing time and productivity dropped when Coach Meadors was replaced by assistant Fred Williams.

After the Olympic break, Swanier didn't play more than 14 minutes in any game and shot 6 of 25 from the field with no three-pointers.

Still, her assist-to-turnover ratio (1.9 to 1.2) was good and her experience valued.

After playing for a year with the Dream, along with a postseason appearance where the team was eliminated by eventual champions, Indiana Fever, in May, 2013, Ketia was released by the Dream. Was *her* dream over?

Ketia holds the championship trophy with Smokey and Rosie

If you ever happen to meet a military brat and happen to let slip the inevitable question; "Where did you come from", be prepared for a lengthy conversation.

—*Military Brat*

Chapter Nine: Playing Abroad

She loves playing in Europe, now; in fact, considers it her second home. But that wasn't always the case.

"My first year overseas was the absolute worst! If you asked me to describe my initial experience playing overseas using one word it would be HOMESICK." She admitted to not even giving it a chance. "I could've been playing in the Caribbean at the time and still felt the same way."

In order to help alleviate her homesickness, she turned to comfort food. Her go-to meals were eggs, bacon, the instant grits her mom sent in care packages, and fast food from McDonald's. She considered herself a *gourmet chef* when cooking boxed mac and cheese, toasting strawberry and s'mores Pop Tarts, and making instant hot chocolate that arrived from the States. Many of the packaged meals she relied on then are, now, a thing of the past, but at the time, the familiar food helped boost her spirits. Playing 007 on her PlayStation also helped during the lonely days she wasn't practicing or playing a basketball game in Rybnik, Poland. "I couldn't have lived without that diversion."

She played in Turkey for a little over two months before returning to Poland. The second time around was so much different from the first. She played in a much nicer city, Gydnia, with a team that had the potential to compete for a Polish Championship. Another crucial difference was her teammates. "I've noticed the winning teams have a better personal connection. They hang out for dinner, for example, and don't just see each other at practice/games. It was nice to be on a team, overseas, that hung out together off the court."

That bond worked to make them so competitive they came in second place that year. Except for one unfortunate incident, they might've come in first. In game two of the finals, Ketia went up for a lay-up, got fouled, and twisted her knee. Although she forced herself to keep playing, she knew something didn't feel right. Plus, the pain was unbearable. Later, tests showed she had injured her MCL (Medial Collateral Ligament) forcing her to leave Poland and go home with only a few weeks left in the season.

While hating to leave in the middle of the tournament, she was relieved her injury wasn't anything more serious. Physical therapy for four weeks was just enough to get her ready for the next year. "I was in physical therapy long enough to recover 100% before leaving for training camp in Gydnia.

The following season, 2012-2013, she played in Israel, the most Americanized country to date. It was a shorter overseas season. (October-March with a super short Christmas break; around four days including travel)

That year, the league made a rule change from allowing three Americans and two Israelis on the court, to four Americans and one Israeli. That didn't sit well with the players or the Israeli fans. The players protested the loss of jobs in their own country by boycotting the league. *No Israeli players no Israeli league.* There were four Americans on Ketia's team and they were the only ones practicing for some weeks. Nobody knew if the season would be cancelled or not. Eventually the league began while keeping the rule change. The Israelis consented to play, despite their dissension. The city in which Ketia played agreed with the protest, however, and forced the team to carry three Americans and two Israelis on the court. As the only team under those restrictions, they were at a disadvantage with the rest of the league.

After Israel, Ketia was back to Poland for five seasons in a row. Having played six years, in five different Polish cities; Rybnik, Gydnia, Szczecin, Polkowice, Sosnowiec, along with a year, each, in Turkey and Israel, she considered herself an Ex-Pat. One of Ketia's most rewarding benefits to playing overseas is the opportunity to travel to different countries and meet people from different cultures. When asked to name a favorite place, she couldn't. "I generally just *love* Europe. The history is incredible. Not one place sticks out because everywhere I visit there's something I love about it. My favorite parts are definitely the views and the amazing architecture; castles, churches, cobblestone streets."

While no specific place was more special than the next, the memory of her mom's first visit was incredibly memorable to both.

Rosie flew to Poland one year during the month of November. Waves of nostalgia rushed through her as she walked through the airport. "I felt I belonged; as if I were returning back from leave when I was in the military." The arrivals area stirred memories of food and miscellaneous items long forgotten. Even the ride back to Ketia's apartment was a thrill because of the years she'd spent in Europe.

Some mornings, after Ketia left for practice, Rosie would find an international breakfast consisting of croissants, a variety of cheeses, cold cuts, coffee and juice waiting for her on the kitchen counter; the typical European morning fare. The gym where her daughter practiced was so close Rosie could see it from the balcony. "Ketia was in a beautiful place not far from shopping, restaurants and grocery stores." After practice mother and daughter had time to take in some of the sites like the waterfront or a bakery that made cupcakes as big as saucers.

"I was so grateful and thankful," Rosie remembered, "for the moments we shared. I knew I would never have those moments again."

Ketia's games were especially exciting. Rosie, along with a gym full of Polish fans, cheered loudly for her. "She played with so much grace. I was ecstatic to have the opportunity to see and share her happy times." Just to know how much her coach believed in her; that Ketia would give her all and play like she belonged, filled her mother with relief and pride. "I call her my ballerina because she creates unbelievable moves in the air. They would make you say out loud, 'Did you see that? Wow.' She is priceless. She is my precious gem."

During that visit Rosie was able to see exactly the way her daughter had grown from the little girl she had taken care of, to the beautiful young lady who was, now, taking care of herself.

"I loved going overseas, and Ketia now understands why I loved being in Europe." Mother and daughter toured Eastern Europe, giving Rosie a chance to revisit places and memories from her military deployments. Both parents knew, however, their daughter's initial dreams could've only been achieved in America.

Her basketball schedule made time at home limited. When she was home, most days were spent with her mom. "I'd be her sous chef in the kitchen, watch TV with her, or just chill and chat. If we weren't home enjoying each other's company, we'd be out running errands."

She remembers the Christmas she and her mom bought Smokey his first set of golf clubs. His face beamed. From that time on, his clubs became his best friends, with golf becoming a positive outlet. When Ketia was home, hanging with her mom, he would be on the course most of the day. Afterward, he would be too tired to hang out, which hurt and confused his daughter. "When I was overseas, phone conversations would be, 'I miss you. I can't wait to see you!' When I was home, I barely saw him."

She felt abandoned, crying over those lost opportunities. During her college years, he'd been her confidant; her second coach. With absolutely no clue as to what was really going on, she only knew her dad wasn't her dad. "I wanted to wrap him in bubble wrap, pack him in a box and send him back to Iraq so they could send back my real dad." Eventually she came to terms with her "new dad" and told herself to "live with it." Only later did she realize the seriousness of his PTSD.

The 2018-2019 Season took her to Hungary, where she played in the small city of Cegled. Settling in with her *globe-trotting poodle*, Roman, the move went smoothly. Throughout the years she'd traveled with him, homesickness, for the most part, was kept at bay. It also helped that Ketia had become a veteran when it came to moving from city to city.

When Ketia found out that close friends of the family, Glen and Annie—also military veterans—wanted to get her a dog to keep her company, she researched, diligently, for small breeds that could easily travel. In addition, she wanted a dog that wouldn't shed and was known to be intelligent and easy to train. Her research led her straight to the toy poodle breed. On her first tour overseas in Poland, she googled toy breeders close to her parent's home. Through a recommendation from a friend, and the generosity of Glen and Annie, she found the perfect match.

Before making a commitment, cautious Ketia asked her mom and dad to check out the breeder and the puppies. The next day she stared, anxiously, at her phone waiting for a call. When her mom's name lit up the screen, she almost dropped the phone trying to answer. Both Rosie and Smokey were at the breeder's home checking on a litter of three available puppies; two girls and one boy. There was no hesitation on Ketia's part. *Roman Swanier* was born November 22, 2008, just for her. She'd always had such a strong love for animals, her aunt was sure she'd be a vet when she grew up. Life and talent took her in a different direction, but Roman filled her need for a companion and best buddy.

Although she began her professional basketball career in America, the majority of the past ten years had been overseas. During time away from practice and games, she got lonely. The pint-size poodle has been the best companion she could ask for. "When we fly, no one even knows he's there. He loves his travel bag," she maintained. "It's his safe haven. He's traveled so much he probably considers it his home." Feedback from other passengers, after nine-hour flights, was usually "shock" that he was on the plane. Their first question was, usually, whether she gave him tranquilizers. "I don't. He's just a great traveler!" He's had two passports, visited more cities/countries, and racked up more airline miles than most humans.

She always feels a certain amount of homesickness whether Roman is with her, or not. His unconditional love, however delivers a huge dose of "medicine" that helps ease the symptoms. For instance, he gives her more responsibility. Instead of staying inside, she has to take him out for bathroom breaks and exercise. That gets her out in the fresh air.

Some teams allowed her to take him on the road and stay in hotels with the players and coaches. "He's the mascot," she bragged. If she can't travel with him, she always finds someone close to the team who enjoys taking care of her low-maintenance poodle.

Roman with his best buddy

Her parents treat Roman like a grandson; especially her mom. Being the smart little poodle, he knows this and uses it to his advantage whenever Ketia visits home. He gives Rosie that "puppy dog look" to get her to cook his favorites—bacon and rice.

He's even been known to fake an injury. Her parents' home has a set of steep stairs. During one visit, Roman limped on one of his back legs for most of the day. Feeling sorry for the little guy, Smokey and Rosie carried him up and down the stairs so his "injured" leg could rest. He thrived on the attention. His limp lasted until he got back to Europe; then disappeared.

When it comes to preparing for another season, enthusiasm is vital to Ketia. It's like hitting the reset button since she usually ends up playing, from one year to the next, with an entirely different team. "You have a very short amount of time to gel, learn your new team mates' style of play, and, sometimes, adjust to a different system with a new coach. You never know from one year to the next what to expect from practices."

She also never knows, from one year to the next, in which country she'll play. It's a waiting game, after each season, whether she'll be in Poland, again, Hungary, Romania, or Israel. Her agent strikes the best deal on the best team available. Once an offer is identified, with Ketia's blessing, a new contract is signed leading to new coaches, new teammates, and a new city or country.

"It's exciting! New opportunities and new cultures. I look forward to it."

While many are resistant to change, Ketia thrives on it and adapts no matter where she lives and plays basketball. *Another benefit of the learning process of an army brat.*

"Not all experiences as a military brat have been filled with sugar and honey

—*Military Brat*

Chapter Ten: The Family Dynamic; PTSD

Only in the past few years has the condition/illness, PTSD, and subsequent treatments, been brought to the forefront by veteran's agencies and health care professionals. It's now thought that more than 15% of veterans return home with some level of the disorder.

The mental and physical damage done to our military, during times of conflict and war, didn't escape Rosie and Smokey Swanier. The collateral damage didn't escape Ketia.

Out of three full years, Smokey was home around seven or eight months. The lack of communication with his family during this time was especially troubling. "After crossing the berm into Iraq for Operation Iraqi Freedom it would be days before I would be able to speak with any of my family. Those were scary times not knowing when and if I would be able to speak with them at all."

His soldiers were stressed, also; the reason he encouraged them to communicate as much as possible. "On the road march to Bagdad," he recalled, "once we met our objectives, we would be able to set up temporarily. The Battalion Communications guy would set up the

SINGARS Radio antenna and I would get a quick call home just to say 'Hello, I love and miss you and everything is fine.' I couldn't talk as long as I would like because there was a possibility I could give away my location and compromise my battalion. Hanging up was tough."

Any call, however, depended on whether he could get in touch with an operator from Fort Benning to connect him to a civilian line. Luckily, a civilian contractor attached to his company had a satellite phone that Smokey and the commander could use from time to time to contact their families. Calling home for just one minute became the norm, but they made the most of it.

The physical pain started a decade earlier in 2002 during *Operation Desert Spring*. It was well known that First Sergeant Swanier was conscientious to a fault, and would never ask his soldiers to do something he wasn't willing to do himself. That work ethic led to a number of slowly debilitating injuries that worsened every year with every deployment.

In 2003, with the 3rd Infantry Division Brigade Combat Team moving across the desert while spearheading the Iraq War, Smokey and his driver encountered a zero-visibility sandstorm causing the **HMMWV (High-Mobility Multipurpose Wheeled Vehicle – also called Humvee)** to hit a sand dune. The impact slammed Smokey's head into the metal stabilizer bar at the top of the vehicle. Add head, neck, and back injury to the chronic pain he was already experiencing.

First Sergeant Swanier and Captain John Argue, had worked closely together during that time, with the commander having a personal view of Smokey's deteriorating mental state. "I could see the pain in his heart was as great as the pain in his body." Not only was the stress of war taking its toll, physically, witnessing the death of a fellow First Sergeant and then two weeks later, the suicide of one of his soldiers, was mentally devastating. Add to that, the additional responsibility for sending those under his charge on dangerous, sometimes deadly, missions.

Smokey's soldier, who committed suicide after redeployment from Kuwait during Operation Desert Spring, was a tragedy all too common among military personnel. In fact, suicidal thoughts are something Smokey, and many veterans deal with on a regular basis. He remembers having just finished Thanksgiving dinner with Rosie and Ketia when he got the call about the suicide. "Devastating, just devastating." The death was even more confusing considering the day before, Smokey had hand-picked him from formation to run PT (Physical Training). "I will never forget how happy he was running that morning." The circumstance and unknown reason behind what led to his suicide continually haunts Smokey.

Another devastating loss was a young soldier, under Smokey's command, whose joyful visit home turned tragic. "I remember releasing my soldiers for their two-week block leave." A week after they all returned home, Smokey received a call that the soldier was killed in a car accident in North Carolina. In a touch of irony, that same soldier was the first to be injured in an accident three hours into the ground war in Iraq.

"I flew to North Carolina for his funeral with three other soldiers to represent our unit. This was already a tough time since we had just arrived back home from Iraq and I was preparing my unit to move forward. The memorial service, complete with bagpipes, was difficult for the family and his fellow soldiers, but our unit helped hold them up."

Smokey admits that it still hurts, today, to think about it. "It's a daily struggle. His memorial was the second of two I had to do during my time as a First Sergeant."

His personal sense of loss is not surprising since, he not only carried a deep concern for, and knowledge of, every one of his soldiers, he knew their family's names as well.

After twenty years of valiant service, Smokey was medically retired due to health issues as the direct result of combat duty. The emotional and physical battles, however, didn't end with Smokey's retirement. They were ongoing. Wanting to spare Ketia, her parents kept her dad's struggles from her. Back then, they didn't fully understand the potential implications of PTSD; flashbacks, insomnia, anger, alcohol or drug abuse, inability to handle social situations, suicidal thoughts, among the symptoms that could arise. How could they burden her?

While Rosie and Smokey struggled to bring normalcy back into their day-to-day lives, Ketia had no clue what had changed or why. "Growing up, I loved being in the gym with my dad. If both of my parents weren't there, it was me and him. He rebounded better than [Chicago Bulls forward, Dennis] Rodman and was always rehabbing my jump shot. 'Follow Through! Jump! There it is!'"

Ketia missed her mentor and gym buddy

During the earlier years, her "gym buddy" could always be counted on 100% of the time. As time passed after college, however, his interest dropped off, significantly. When asked to assess her jump shot, or play some one-on-one, he'd answer, "Not today," or, "Ask your mom."

Eventually, Ketia stopped asking. "I felt like a kid who lost her favorite teddy bear. Gym time wasn't the same. Losing Dad's training and instruction forced me to rehab my shot on my own while imagining his words in my head, 'Follow Through! Jump! There it is!'"

Despite being kept out of the loop, Ketia was acutely aware something was wrong. Her frustration deepened as Smokey's symptoms worsened. During conversations with her mom, Rosie did her best to explain that Smokey's issues were severe, triggering his growing need for solitude. That still wasn't enough for Ketia. Her lack of knowledge about the syndrome and how severe/traumatic was Smokey's case, caused her, at the time, to reject any feeling of understanding or empathy.

For Smokey, the process of healing was, and still is, slow and tortuous. When he returned from Iraq in 2003, all he could think about was spending time with his family, but once he landed, it all felt empty. "Getting off of the plane, and getting on a bus to get back to my unit. Anxiety, anxiety, anxiety!"

His mind rushed; focused on getting home even though he knew, before he could personally go anywhere, he had to account for all of the unit's weapons, weapons systems, radios, etc.

As Rosie remembers, all seemed good when Smokey first came home from Iraq. The relief to have him, once more, part of the family unit, was everything she'd imagined and hoped for during his, and her, years of service and deployment. It wasn't long, however, before she noticed changes in his demeanor, his tone of voice, and even the way he spoke to her, or rather *at* her.

Not one to suppress her feelings, she'd ask, "What's going on with you?" He'd snap back, "What are you talking about?" After it happened a few more times she knew something was wrong because he'd never, in all their years of marriage, spoken to her in such an angry tone. As with most PTSD sufferers, he was in consistent denial that his tone was negative or any different than it had ever been. Rosie persisted, and strongly suggested he get help. Still, he continued denying that changes in his behavior were, in any way, affecting him and the family. That denial would be seriously tested during a visit with his dad.

After the death of Smokey's mother, Corena, his father, Adrian, traveled around the country for a few months visiting children and grandchildren. During a stay with Rosie and Smokey in Georgia, father and son decided to go out for a few hours on their own. From Smokey's perspective, their time together went well, but during their return home, Adrian asked, "Son, why are you so argumentative now?" That floored Smokey, because Rosie had, repeatedly, asked the same question since his return from Iraq; constantly insisting something was "just not right with me."

His father, an educator for over 35 years, had never judged others and was known as a good listener. "I could go to my dad—any of us could—and if you told him, 'I made a mistake,' he would say, 'Son, the only person I know who hasn't made a mistake is a person who hasn't done anything.' He was that type of person. He would have an answer for everything and tell you why." If Adrian noticed a difference in his son, Smokey would have to face facts.

That Saturday morning, he was in the Atlanta Veteran's Administration in front of the Director of the *Post Combat Traumatic Program*. After the interview, Smokey agreed to enroll in a sixteen-week treatment session even though he was still convinced he didn't need to be there. Just like an alcoholic or drug addict, he refused to accept responsibility. "To this day I remember thinking that first session was much too long. I also remember the day I finished the sixteen-week outpatient program and thinking it was not nearly long enough."

He was the first *Operation Iraqi Freedom* veteran to attend that particular outpatient program. Most participants were Vietnam War veterans. After listening to their stories, and what they'd gone through just to get to that point, made Smokey realize how fortunate he was to get treatment in such a timely manner. He discovered new battle buddies from a different battle field.

With them, he learned how to share through tears and pain. The first step was to define the symptoms of Post-Traumatic Stress Disorder and then learn how to deal. They made tapes, about their feelings, frustrations, and emotional distress, and then listened to them. Another exercise was to put their thoughts on a piece of paper and then burn it in the woods.

Three hours a day, three days a week for sixteen weeks, he not only shared what he was going through but listened to what every Vietnam Veteran had to share. "This was life changing in a way that I still share to this day," he affirmed.

In the process, Smokey made one personal friend, Harry Stokes, who has become such a cornerstone in his life through sharing combat and military experiences that Rosie and Ketia call him *Uncle Harry*.

The couple also had the opportunity to attend a transcendental meditation class to help both of them deal with the stress and the symptoms of PTSD.

After finishing with the sixteen-week outpatient program, he continues to see, on a regular basis, the same doctor who interviewed him at the VA that first Saturday morning.

"It has been a challenge and continues to be a challenge as I go through life. I also take the opportunity to speak with fellow soldiers who deployed with me and are going through the same thing as well. There are two days I no longer worry about; yesterday and tomorrow. I take life one day at a time."

"Our character is built as our lives progress, our weaknesses exposed as we face difficulty, and our willingness to succeed unearthed as we overcome adversity."
—*Military Brat*

Chapter Eleven: Rosie's Surgery and Recovery

Adding more strain to the family unit, Rosie was diagnosed with a .7cmm brain tumor in 2014. "Before my diagnosis, I was normal. At least I thought I was. I did everything I wanted to do. I was living a great life." It was great until she went to bed one Saturday night in the summer of 2014 and woke up Sunday morning with a painless lump on the side of her neck. Smokey felt the lump and immediately said, "You need to go and get it checked out." She made an appointment the next day.

Although a blood test came back negative, the doctor suggested Rosie get a CT scan. Heeding the advice, she called right away to schedule an appointment for the following Friday morning. After the scan, she hadn't been home ten minutes before getting called back to the doctor. A very anxious couple drove straight to the office and received the news that a large mass was on her brain. She cried for two or three minutes and then put her situation in God's hands.

To all three Swaniers, this health crisis hit like a cruel twist of fate. Certain, at that time, she'd lost the dad she once knew, Ketia couldn't bear the thought of losing her mother. Rosie was the cushion, the sounding board, the buffer. She was the one person who understood Smokey and his condition and stood between her husband and possible conflict with himself or others. Ketia also feared that her dad wouldn't be able to go on without his wife of more than thirty years. He'd had previous suicidal thoughts, and she couldn't see him surviving without his partner in career and life. After all, Rosie was the rock, the glue that held them together.

Ketia recalls the day her dad gave her the news about the health challenge that faced her mother.

"I was eating lunch with some friends when I got a call from my dad."

"Hey Dad!"

"Hey Keesh, are you busy?"

"Just having lunch with some friends. What's up?"

She listened to Smokey's news and then excused herself from the table to get more information outside. She was emotionless at first. She couldn't believe her ears. When she told her dad she'd be home that night or the next day, he calmly told her it didn't have to be that soon and he would let her know the surgery date as soon as he found out. When she choked up, he reassured her that everything would be alright. She hung up, walked back in the restaurant, and rejoined her friends as if she'd just received an everyday business call. The moment she got home, she broke down. It would be some time after her mother's surgery before she returned to being "okay".

Always there for each other

Rosie's surgeon had to make some medium incisions in her head to remove her tumor. As a consequence, her head had to be shaven. "Mom was not on board at all," Ketia chuckled. Dad and I made a pact that we would both shave our heads for mom's cause. When she was admitted into the hospital before surgery, all three of us were bald and beautiful."

When Ketia was home for the surgery, she was aware her dad had PTSD but still unaware of its seriousness. She did know he was dealing with something deeper than she could understand. "I was more worried about him than Mom during her surgery and recovery. The tumor covered her frontal lobe and would involve a very serious operation. If I lost my mom, I felt I would lose my dad, too. I wanted to be the strong one for all of us." She tried to hold back tears but cried one last time before Rosie got wheeled off to surgery.

The next seven hours of waiting felt like days as Ketia fought not to worry. While Ketia and her dad were the only family allowed to visit Rosie right after surgery, they had plenty of company in the waiting room. All Rosie's brothers, sisters-in-law, and brothers-in-law were there for support. As it turned out, the surgery went smoothly. Although Rosie wasn't aware of anything at the time, her husband and daughter repeated over and over how much they loved her.

After being thoroughly checked following a couple of unexpected seizures, Rosie was finally able to go home. Possibly to release frustrations at not being able to communicate for a while, unpleasant hospital food, a stream of doctors in and out her room, Ketia caught her mom strolling down the hallway at home, with the help of her walker, joyfully singing Pharrell Williams lyrics, 'Because I'm happy,' like a broken record. "I walked behind tracing her steps with a large smile on my face knowing, at that moment, she would be okay."

Before and after the surgery and months of recuperation, Ketia moved into the role of buffer between her dad and the world. But, how do you help someone when you don't really understand the problem?

For example, Ketia had taken careful notes and instructions from the hospital about her mother's rehabilitation process. Smokey didn't agree with the method. His way was better. "But, Dad, I was there and heard exactly what we should do," carried no weight with the former First Sergeant. After years of being responsible for his soldiers, he now carried the complete, self-imposed burden of taking command of his wife's recovery. While his attitude appeared like "Captain of the World" syndrome, he was simply reverting back to war time and taking his wife's health issues and recovery on his shoulders. One of the heartbreaking problems for military veterans and their families is the inability to slide back into civilian and domestic life. Panic and the fear that someone will die under their "watch" is ever-present.

Ketia struggled, mightily, to understand, but with little knowledge of the cause of her dad's mental state, she became more confused as the weeks progressed. "After I knew Mom was going to be okay, I couldn't wait to get back to Poland. The stress of dealing with my mother's surgery and my dad's emotional instability was too much." The everyday challenge of basketball practice and the upcoming season was a welcome relief.

"I just thought, for years, my dad didn't want to be around me," she recently confessed. "It's only been in the past year he's talked to me about what he's going through." The barrier didn't break until she was around twenty-nine. "I don't remember what caused it to break but it did. I started asking my dad more PTSD specific questions and he began opening up a lot more about his issues. It helped me tremendously with understanding the 'why' behind his distance."

Those conversations helped mend the chasm that had, for years, festered between father and daughter. The recent communication also took strain off the family. Smokey and Rosie no longer feel burdened to pretend everything is fine. The whole family now works as a team to cope with the personal rigors of life-long veteran rehabilitation.

Small wonder Smokey, and so many other veterans, finds integrating back into society and even their own family units so difficult. Vivid memories of war, responsibility for hundreds of soldiers, and death, along with an unexpected family health crisis, proved overpowering to First Sergeant Swanier. While he has now acknowledged, and is getting medical help and mental health counseling for his diagnosed, PTSD, he fights war-related demons on a regular basis.

Decades in the military brought both mental and physical pain, however, he proudly states one statistic. "I took 216 soldiers to war and brought 216 soldiers back."

To this day, the couple is dedicated to exercise. Between bike riding, yoga, and weight training, they recognize the value gained in maintaining their mental and physical health.

Education is the most powerful weapon which you can use to change the world"
—Nelson Mandela

Chapter Twelve: Ketia4Kidz

Ketia4Kidz Foundation began in 2008 to inspire military brats worldwide to pursue their dreams in life and to help them overcome the problems created from being the children of military parents. Most "brats" have only one parent in the military, which is a challenge in itself, but Ketia is doubly qualified since her mom and dad both served at the same time.

Despite this, she overcame obstacles through hard work, dedication, and support from her family. Also, a passion for sports helped her focus on education and athletics while growing up in a single parent household due to deployments and military duties. This focus created hard work and determination that drove her to believe and pursue her dreams to become a professional basketball player.

Ketia was inspired by her own story to inspire kids from similar backgrounds. Finding a passion, becoming determined, and having tremendous support, helped her reach her goals. Growing up as a military brat, and being an only child with both parents in the army, made clear the focus of her foundation.

So many factors tie in to why military brats show resiliency through childhood. Those same factors also play a role in why military brats struggle with certain life issues as well. Considering her struggles and successes throughout the years, Ketia related to both the positive and negative characteristics of the children whose lives mirrored her own. "I wore the exact same shoes my first eighteen years of life."

Her parents played a major role when it came to creating the foundation, from helping brainstorm, to 501(c) 3 non-profit paperwork, to helping choose scholarship recipients. "They've been here since day one and continue to be a huge support system, not only with the foundation, but in my life in general." She's quick to praise her father's administrative role. He is her right hand when it comes to running it. It's certain in her mind the foundation wouldn't be where it is today, without his vision.

In the **Ketia4Kidz Foundation** early years, there was no real structure. Ketia knew she wanted to give back to that specific community, but saw no clear path to accomplish her goal. Starting small by hosting ice cream socials, led to visiting schools, and hosting military families at her WNBA games. As time went on, the *Adrian & Corena Swanier Education Scholarship* was established, and the main focus of the foundation, created.

The largest fundraising event is an annual charity golf outing, usually held in April at the Mirror Lake Country Club, in Villa Rica, GA. Sponsors and golfers from all over the country participate in an 18-hole event in the West Georgia Mountains.

The only thing more plentiful than prizes, are the volunteers.

Dozens of friends and family members have pitched in to make the event successful, year after year, beginning with a military salute by all participants.

There are 1.7 million American children and youth under 18 with a parent serving in the military and about 900,000 with one or both parents deployed multiple times. April is designated as the Month of the Military Child, underscoring the important role military children play in the armed forces community. It's an opportunity to recognize military children and youth for their heroism, character, courage, sacrifices and continued resilience.

The golf outing became an annual tradition the year after the scholarship program started. While this annual event has awarded over $56,000 in scholarship funds since its inception in 2010, the goal is to raise as much money as possible to **Ketia4Kidz** until, eventually, a $5,000 scholarship will be awarded to each recipient. Starting in 2019 the program has sponsored sixteen recipients, all of whom will receive scholarship money until they graduate, as long as the re-application guidelines are followed.

In 2018, April tradition was broken with a 10-year **Ketia4Kidz** foundation anniversary celebration golf outing. *A Tribute to Military Brats*, was held in Orlando, Florida, May 11-13 in order to honor the many volunteers throughout the years.

The foundation wanted to, not only, celebrate military brats during the annual golf outing, but to also show appreciation to donors and sponsors. Over the ten years of existence, participants have traveled from at least twenty-five different states to support the fundraiser that began when Ketia played her first years in the WNBA. As in past years, traditional golf was the main focus of the festivities, with food and entertainment plentiful after the charity event.

"When we started out, we never envisioned the fundraiser growing as large as it did, with as many college scholarships being handed out," Smokey stated. "We are very proud of what she has accomplished; especially having achieved so much from afar. She's been such an inspiration for so many children, especially from the military community."

The Adrian & Corena Swanier Education Scholarship was named after Ketia's paternal grandparents, Adrian and Corena Swanier; both educators and mentors in their Mississippi community for over 30 years. Every summer her AAU basketball team competed in a national tournament hosted in a different state. Adrian and Corena attended every year. Their support, love and inspiration, helped empower Ketia to be the person she is today. "They left footprints on my life, forever."

These scholarships provide a lifeline for students who might not be able to achieve their dreams of studying biomedical sciences, graphic design, music, or environmental science.

Testimonials from scholarship recipients:

"This scholarship will help me pay for a quality undergraduate degree that I can use to succeed on the LSAT."

"Obtaining a college education wouldn't have been possible without the Adrian & Corena Swanier Education Scholarship."

"I feel this scholarship will help me realize an opportunity I felt I did not have a few years ago. I always felt that I would not be able to function in the world with my autism. Now, I can see a different future and this scholarship will help me get that much closer."

"This scholarship will help me to breathe easier, live and eat!"

"The cost of college tuition is a large weight not just on me, but on the whole family. This scholarship will go a long way towards alleviating that weight."

Several other organizations have jumped on the bandwagon to further this worthy cause. The Connecticut Sun sold tickets to a game with the Washington Mystics at the Mohegan Sun Arena to benefit Ketia4Kidz. Fans could purchase the special ticket package for themselves or for donation to a military family and then a special meet and greet with Ketia was set up prior to the game.

Amazon recently added the charity to their *Smile* donation program.

Ketia doesn't just *talk the talk*. She also *walks the walk* with a mentoring program. "I enjoy getting to know a little bit about the recipients and doing something for them each year that will give them additional fuel to their already motivated fire to reach their short- and long-term goals."

She also encourages every recipient to keep a *Passion Planner* that helps individuals "stay focused, create your passion, see the big picture, challenge yourself," among others. "I want to make sure they are putting their passion planners to use."

For the past few years, she has purchased *Passion Planners* for each recipient. "I want to inspire them to continue to stay on track and help show them how far they've grown each month." Each week the journal breaks down your personal to-do and work goals and gives positive quotes. At the end of each month, you're asked the same seven questions so you can reflect back. One of the requirements for their Ketia4kidz re-application is to send four different answers from the seven questions to show passion planners are being put to use, and answers, valued. Each month, a recipient shares the experience in the Brats Blog on the foundation website.

Tracy Barnett (pictured above), who began her medical rotations in November, 2017, wrote in her planner:

This past month, I started my clinical rotations for Medical-Surgical (Med-Surg). This was the most memorable moment of not just this past month, but of the semester so far. I shadowed nurses for a total of 48 hours on a telemetry unit of a hospital and it was great. The experience was tiring, I'm not going to lie, but I learned a lot and I enjoyed myself. We were each assigned a patient each week and got to practice writing care plans, making prep forms, and report sheets.

Ketia hopes these exercises will keep the dedication and enthusiasm for education first and foremost in the minds of scholarship recipients.

When many think of military sacrifice, they think of men and women on the battlefield willing to sacrifice their lives, often forgetting about the people that those men and women leave at home." –

—*Military Brat*

Chapter Thirteen: Future of Ketia4Kidz Foundation

*K*etia's plans for the future.

"I want to continue to provide a positive impact in at least one student a year. If Ketia4Kidz can accomplish more than one; even better. Since I'm rarely home, what my family and I have been able to accomplish yearly, with the help of our amazing support system, is truly incredible. My father and I connect pretty well, considering we're 'oceans apart' most of the year.

The feedback I receive from the recipients, and the extremely hard work they put in, gives me the energy to continue to help other military children the best way I can. Each year they've been given different tasks to re-apply for their scholarship. The majority of recipients do re-apply. It's been really cool to have the same recipients throughout their entire college career.

I've also had the satisfaction of seeing recipients graduate and make their dreams a reality. Ketia4Kidz isn't about me. I never want any credit for the non-profit. It was created to help give back and have an impact on the lives of others. I want it to continue to do just that."

(The 2020 and 2021 tournaments were cancelled due to Covid restrictions. The Ketiz4Kidz Charity Golf Tournament will resume in 2022)

Meet four of the Adrian & Corena Swanier Scholarship Recipients:

In 2018 the **Ketia4Kidz Foundation** celebrated their 10 Year Anniversary and continued commitment to inspire military brats worldwide to pursue their dreams in life. We continue to exist because of your support and generous donation. I can't tell you how much your support is appreciated. Our goal is to provide support for military brats through our Adrian and Corena Swanier Scholarship program. We provided 11 scholarships in 2017, 15 scholarships in 2018, and plan to grow every year. Your donation allows scholarship recipients to progress in their educational dream. We're making a difference in their lives and pursuit for higher learning.

***California Lutheran University Major: Communication Goals:* Gabriela Flores** wants to work with either a television company or film studio as a graphic designer and video scripter.

"The Adrian and Corena Swanier Education Scholarship will help me continue at California Lutheran University which I believe is the perfect fit for me - fulfilling my dream of playing soccer at the college level while receiving an outstanding education in the field of communication."

***Alabama A&M University Major: Mechanical Engineering Goals:* Diondre Bell** wants to work for NASA or the military involving engineering.

"Thank you everyone involved with this program and for selecting me as a recipient. This has honestly helped me get to college, and I truly appreciate all that y'all have done for me and military brats worldwide."

***University of Maryland Major: General Biology Goals:* Sophia Walsh** wants to attend dental school and become an orthodontist.

"This scholarship will help make the long road to becoming an orthodontist achievable."

***University of North Texas Major: Anthropology:* Sarah Richardson** enjoys reading, cooking, yoga and writing. "With this scholarship, I can pay for my classes without taking out a loan!"

**Ketia's extended family
Uncle Victor, Aunt Daphne,
Uncle Chief, Grandma Corena, Papoo,
and Uncle Red**

Epilogue: A Message from Ketia
The revolving door

    Young heroes endure sacrifices because one or both parent(s) sacrificed their life for America's freedom while serving in the United States Armed Forces. These unique sacrifices teach perseverance by overcoming individual challenges they face. These heroes are Military Brats.

    We fight the same war, on different battlefields, conquering the same enemies

Afghanistan soldiers meet with former NBA/WNBA players

I want to thank, and honor, all Military Brats for their sacrifices. I am a military brat who came into this world having both parents work for the United States Army. Cornell and Rosie Swanier served America for 22 1/2 years. If I wasn't moving from state to state, I was moving to another country and then back to the states. A parent would deploy, return home in order to deploy again, and then come back so the other parent could deploy. Sometimes life resembled a revolving door.

There are times I forget where I was born, but I *never* forget how the military life played a significant role in the person I am today. It built a persevering character that led me to my dreams of becoming a professional basketball player. A crystal ball couldn't have predicted an ARMY Brat would receive a full scholarship to play basketball at The University of Connecticut (UCONN), get drafted in the Women's National Basketball Association (WNBA) first round of my class, win a WNBA championship, and play professional basketball in Europe.

We (military brats) have different stories that share the same chapters. I share my story to inform other military brats that their challenges help shape who they are today. Believe me, it's not always easy, but we find a way. We are proud, resilient, strong, adaptable heroes who wouldn't change our childhoods for the world.

Always work extremely hard to reach your goals. Once you reach those goals, you have to continue working harder and harder. Believe in yourself, be yourself, and be kind to one another.

Enjoy and keep inspiring.

Love, from one military brat to another.

Ketia Swanier

"Love for basketball comes naturally when you're born in Indiana."

Mary Cunningham, a Southern Indiana native and sports junkie, was compelled to share the life story of Ketia Swanier, military brat, AAU player, high school star, UConn guard, and WNBA champion.

Ghost Light, a memoir-based fictional short story, about a boy's adventure watching the Chicago Cubs from the window in his grandmother's Brownstone apartment, is published in the Mystery Readers Journal, Sports Mysteries, Vol. 25, #4.

The author also writes adult mysteries, middle-grade time-travel fantasy, and women's lifestyle/humor.

She is a member of Sisters in Crime, International, Sisters in Crime-Atlanta Chapter, International Thriller Writers, Inc., and the Carrollton Writers Guild.

Ms. Cunningham enjoys golf, swimming, and exploring the mountains of West Georgia where she makes her home with her husband and adopted, four-legged, furry daughter, Lucy.

http://www.marycunninghambooks.com

www.ingramcontent.com/pod-product-compliance
Lightning Source LLC
Chambersburg PA
CBHW072028110526
44592CB00012B/1427